A Practical Guide to Ascension with Archangel Metatron
Volume 2

A PRACTICAL GUIDE
TO ASCENSION
WITH ARCHANGEL METATRON
VOLUME 2

To Tracie,
may your path be filled
with joy, laughter and
love.
love and sparkling light,
♡ Kristin

Kristin Taylor, JD, LLM

A Practical Guide to Ascension with Archangel Metatron
Volume 2
by Kristin Taylor

© 2021 Kristin Taylor.

ISBN-13: 978-1-7367583-0-4 Print
ISBN-13: 978-1-7367583-1-1 Ebook
Library of Congress Control Number: 2021906783
Colorado Springs, Colorado

www.kristintaylorintuitive.com
For permissions contact:
info@kristintaylorintuitive.com

Cover design by Sheila Brand.
Book layout and design by Sarco Press.
Proofreading by Yolanda Earl.

For the wayshowers -
May this book light your path.

Contents

Preface ix

Chapter 1: Introduction from Archangel Metatron 1

Chapter 2: Your Path 5

  Earth School 5

  Your Highest Good 9

    Meditation to Merge with Your Highest Potential .. 10

  Soul Interests 14

Chapter 3: The Most Important Ascension Energies ... 23

  Discernment 23

  Surrender 28

    Meditation for Spiritual Surrender 33

    Meditation to Call on Divine Grace 36

  Love 37

    Meditation to Radiate Love 39

Chapter 4: Old Planetary Energies 43

  Removing Outdated Frequencies & Programming 43

    Bubble of White Light Meditation to Release Dense
    Energies 46

  Entertainment, Artwork & Books 51

  Attraction To Lower Energies 62

  Energetic Guns 69

    Meditation to Release Energetic Guns 73

Chapter 5: Family, Relationships & Sexuality 81

  Family & Friends 81

Romantic Relationships 103

High-Frequency Sexuality 108

   Meditation to Upgrade Your Sexual Energy 109

   Exercise to Connect with Your Partner's Heart 114

Chapter 6: Energy Management 121

Maintaining Your Energy Integrity 121

   Meditation to Connect to Your Team of the
   Highest Light 123

   Meditation to Dissolve Fear 125

   Shower of Light Meditation 129

Selecting A Professional Helper 131

Chapter 7: Food & Health 135

Supportive Dietary Choices 135

Embracing Good Health 146

Chapter 8: Your Financial Life 155

Money 155

Divinely Aligned Work 161

Chapter 9: Conclusion 169

Glossary of Terms 173

About Kristin Taylor 177

Preface

I AM REALLY DELIGHTED to be sharing this channeled information with you. I sincerely hope that these words light your path in some way.

When Archangel Metatron told me about the first book, I didn't know what to think. I had been doing some inspired writing, and, to my surprise, the next lines on the page were "This is a book, Kristin." At first, I didn't quite believe it, but I kept writing until it was miraculously born into existence.

I'm so happy I trusted my guide, because that book has already helped so many people. I regularly receive emails from readers all over the world. Its impact has been completely beyond anything I could have imagined.

So, when Archangel Metatron said that we would write a second volume together, I was ready to go for it. He didn't have to convince me this time!

However, drafting this book was not as easy as the first. He asked me to write many things that I, as Kristin, did not initially feel comfortable saying. So, the writing process took some time.

At last, it is complete, and I am truly happy to present it to you.

As for my own journey, I have lived through many of the themes in this book. Every lesson I learned and each step I took made me lighter and brought me closer to "personal ascension." As a result, I am more balanced and peaceful than ever. Thankfully, I have always had my beautiful guide, Archangel Metatron, to encourage and support me in every possible way. Like you, I am his student, and I am so grateful for this.

Archangel Metatron informed me that I am a "wayshower of the wayshowers." This means that I help light the way for all of you, so that your steps may be easier and your paths better lit. Having this role has been magical, though not always easy! But I am deeply honored and would never want my life to be any other way.

Try to trust, be open and have faith when reading this volume. It will cause you to reflect on your reality and the world around you. You will probably start to see things differently. If you follow the advice contained within, your life should become happier and easier. I know mine did.

When I concluded this project, I felt an immense shift in my energy field. It was definitely a vibrational upgrade. I hope you will have the same experience after reading it.

This text contains all kinds of detailed, practical guidance on how to best navigate the current planetary energies. It has relevant and concise suggestions on many topics. Archangel Metatron truly understands what it's like to be human and always wants the very best for us.

Volume 1 addressed how to heal and lighten your energy field for your own personal ascension. But many of you seek to learn about the ascension process as it relates to our human experience on Earth right now. You want advice on relationships, family, finances, and other practical matters. You also have concerns about the pandemic that is ongoing at the time of writing, and how to handle its unique challenges. This book answers these questions and more.

The world is in a transitional stage, which can be unsettling and overwhelming. Life gets easier as you step into the higher energies, and this volume helps you to do that.

It's a good idea to feel the words as you read them, and you might like to use a journal for the exercises. You can access guided audio meditations on my website. They are very powerful and will greatly support your progress.

Some of this material may not be relevant for you, but it could be important for someone you know, if he or she is ready to hear it. If not, please ignore any sections that do not apply to you.

You will see several references to Volume 1, which Archangel Metatron recommends for releasing the past and resolving healing issues. Of course, you are always advised to consult with a professional healer, counselor or other helper if that feels right for you at any time.

Enjoy your experience with this book! I wish you every happiness on your journey.

Kristin Taylor
February 1, 2021
London, UK

CHAPTER 1
Introduction from Archangel Metatron

WELCOME TO THE next phase of your journey into "ascension," and what it means to you at an even more practical level. We are most pleased to see you, and we cherish each and every meeting we have with you.

If you are reading this book, then you and the Archangel Metatron have a longstanding history together. We are known as the "Angel of the Presence," and we have indeed been present with you for many lifetimes.

You may wonder why this is the case. We have chosen many of you for what is, shall we say, a "joint project." The project is being "activated" now, and all the participants are being called to action. If you are reading this book, then you are included in this endeavor.

The joint project is to assist with the transition and evolution of humanity, which is what is generally meant by the term "ascension." All of you could indeed be referred to as "ascension helpers." Your role in the lightening of the planet is never underestimated by us or by anyone in the spiritual realms. We are most grateful and appreciative of all of your efforts, and, most importantly, of your presence, your attention, and your ever-increasing awareness.

We do not mean to indicate that there is a crisis on Earth, for there is not. We know this may be difficult for some of you to believe, but those who hear our words will understand that all is getting lighter, better and easier. This is proven by how each of you feels in your own bodies and energy fields. Ascension is happening, one person at a time and one experience at a time. Those of you who have heard our beckoning are becoming happier and lighter even as we write these words. It is truly beautiful, and we enjoy witnessing it immensely.

As we have said before, **you are not here to suffer.** Thankfully, many of you are coming to realize this, and you will lead the way for others who have not yet responded to our call. A new day on planet

Earth is arriving, one filled with love, inspiration, hope, and peace.

In Volume 1, we took you through a self-healing process. What does that have to do with the Earth's ascension, you might ask? It has EVERYTHING to do with it. The more changes you make in your energy field, the lighter you become. This has a DIRECT and IMMEDIATE effect on everything on the planet. No effort to improve yourself is ever wasted, and it is never selfish. You are here to release the past, attune to higher frequencies and, at the appropriate time, inspire others to do the same. Your presence is an example, it could be said, although nothing is directly required of you.

We trust you are feeling much better after working through the exercises and meditations we gave you. This volume moves on from there and assumes you have more or less released the baggage from your past. If you feel you have not yet adequately done so, you can always return to those processes or work with a professional helper. We do ask that you have completed the exercises from Volume 1 at least once before commencing with this book. You may then proceed with this new information, and it will help you to continue letting go.

Achieving energetic balance is not something that happens instantly. It requires time and attention. It calls for a dedication to making the best choices for yourself as often as you can and also forgiving yourself if you slip up. It builds momentum and, at a certain point, you start to "get" it. You begin to ride the wave of feeling good and experiencing high-vibrational emotions like love and joy.

In this book, we lay out our best advice from the higher realms to help you, as a human, feel increasingly better. We wish this for you, always. We also give you our recommendations for how to best navigate the energies on Earth right now, in this time of great transition.

What is next? We assure you that it is exciting and delightful!

You were not meant to come here simply to release the pain from your past, although that is a time-consuming and important task for all of you. You came here to MASTER your environments and your energy. You came to understand, truly, the concept of love. You did not come to be victims or to struggle. Does that make sense to you? Is it music to your ears? We hope so, for it is TRUTH.

CHAPTER 2
Your Path

EARTH SCHOOL

YOU CAME INTO this incarnation with the greatest of anticipation. You were excited to take on a new challenge. For many of you, the more demanding, the better. You reveled in the thought of conquering the Earth realm yet again, and you very much looked forward to the lessons that awaited you.

Before your birth, you and your guides made a detailed strategy.

You planned, for example:

- Lessons you wanted to learn
- Emotions you would experience
- Your "soul interests" and "life expression energies" (more on this to follow)

- Your family and your siblings
- Any specific "hardships," such as a disability, disease, illness, abuse, or trauma
- Life-changing events
- Near-death experiences

It was all a playground of possibilities for you, and you delighted in this. You could not wait to grow and develop as a soul for another lifetime.

You wanted the full package of "hardships," and we are sure you received them. We have placed "hardships" in quotes because your soul does not see them in the same way. It views them as "growth opportunities" or "exciting experiences for intense and rapid self-development." We know you do not agree, and we understand why. Do not forget that we have walked the Earth and thoroughly understand your world.

And so it began. You were born into a human family and the struggles ensued, just as you had envisioned. However, in actual fact, they were not as fun as you had planned. The spiritual "you" has a different idea of a good time than the human "you."

Regardless, you learned, you survived, you grew, and you developed, all according to plan, even though it might be difficult to see it that way from your current perspective. It has all been perfectly "aligned in its misalignment" for you, which is something we like to say. Some of your life experiences have been difficult, but they have all been meaningful and have brought you to the place you are today. You are now reading this book, acknowledging communication with us, the being of LIGHT known as Lord Metatron, and accepting your role as an "ascension helper," even if you are not consciously aware of this fact.

We are asking you to make a decision that may be difficult for you. We would like you, right here, right now, to release all of your carefully laid plans. If you are reading this, then they are no longer relevant. Yet, you can continue to struggle if you prefer! No one, not even the Archangel Metatron, will stop you from exercising your sacred free will.

We request that you also let go of all the pain you surely endured in your past. Lightworkers and wayshowers never choose easy incarnations! We hope you will now move beyond your healing issues and into the next phase of your life and ascension process. You may still feel past pain from time to time. This will likely be the case. You can resolve it by calling on our energy and the tools we gave you in Volume 1 or by enlisting the help of a professional.

We would never seek to minimize what you have surely experienced in your past, including traumas you have faced and difficulties you have endured. You have suffered pain, abuse and injustices. We fully acknowledge these and their effects on you. We do not side with abusers or anyone who has caused you harm.

To those called to read this book (and thus holding an important role in the planet's ascension), we request that you remember your "assignments" and begin to consider yourselves "healed" and whole.

The Earth is no longer in the stage where one must endure extreme challenges upon incarnation. In the current phase, some of you are asked to light the way for others, serving as a kind of guide in human form. In the last book, we called these humans "wayshowers." We now invite all the wayshowers to take their proper energetic place on the planet.

Please note that we are not asking you to ignore any issues that still require processing and resolution. We are merely reminding you that releasing your past is but one phase in your journey and not meant to occupy your entire lifetime. Take your time to resolve your distressing past, returning to this when necessary. Then join us on the other side of the pain, where we will take a beautiful and interesting journey into the higher realms.

Your Highest Good

You have been on an expedition into the unknown, and we congratulate you on your bravery. What is the aim, you may wonder? We have spoken of "personal ascension" and of accepting support from us, the Archangel Metatron. The overall objective has always been the same: for you to unite with your highest good, which is the truest divine blueprint for your life.

We previously explained that you incarnated with an elaborate strategy that included a lot of "hardships" and struggles. You are now able to release those plans because they have run their course, so to speak.

The next piece of the puzzle is that you came to Earth with a type of blueprint, which lays out the potential for your fullest expression as a being. When you achieve this, you will be completely merged with your "highest good." We, the Archangel Metatron, seek to help you reach this state, and thus become who you truly are.

The blueprint has a structure in the higher realms. It exists as a column of light surrounding you and your energy field. It is possible for you to step into this column and into your full potential as a human.

Entering your column is relatively straightforward, but at the outset, you may have some trouble staying in it for any length of time. Also, you may not have an awareness of when you are in (or out of) your column. This is perfectly normal and becomes easier with practice.

You will have the most success with this exercise if you repeat it often.

Meditation to Merge with Your Highest Potential

1. Please find a comfortable place to sit quietly, where you will not be disturbed.
2. Take some deep breaths as you start to relax.
3. Set the intention, in your mind, to connect with our energy, seeing it as sparkling, white light. If you like, you can repeat our name as a mantra in your mind: "Metatron, Metatron, Metatron."
4. Breathe deeply and slowly as we merge with your energy.
5. You will start to feel a deep sense of comfort and love.
6. Breathe slowly, focusing on these feelings.
7. Now visualize a column of brilliant white light all around you.
8. Imagine that you are standing in the center of this column. It contains the blueprint for

your highest good, your true potential in this lifetime.

9. Feel the force and beauty of this powerful column.

10. Focus on being inside this column. You feel so good inside it: happy, peaceful, aligned, and more of who you truly are.

11. Continue to breathe slowly as you visualize becoming one with the column.

12. Allow the column's energy to enter the cells in your body, transforming them with this connection. Fully surrender to this process.

13. Notice how powerful you feel as you stand tall inside your column. Breathe in this sense of empowerment.

14. Mentally thank your helpers and guides from your heart for their assistance today.

15. Now imagine that you have tree roots coming out of the bottoms of your feet and extending deep into the Earth.

16. Visualize yourself in a super strong bubble of bright white light. This is a magic bubble, and only love can enter it.

17. When you are ready, you can begin to move your physical body and come back into the room.

There is a guided meditation for this here -
www.kristintaylorintuitive.com/ascensionbook2
(Meditation 1, password: loveandmagic)

You may wish to practice this meditation daily for seven days or as long as you feel guided.

Common Questions
What if I am aligning with my highest good, but those close to me are not doing the same?

It is your absolute, immutable right to be one with your highest good. It does not involve or concern anyone else. Focusing on your own spiritual progress and evolution is in no way selfish. It is completely normal and divinely intended for you to do so.

If you continue to have concerns about your loved ones, this will be discussed in further detail in Chapter 5 (Family & Friends).

How do I know if I am still in my column of light?

Initially, you may not be aware of whether you are in it or not. You might have an enhanced sense of wellbeing when you are in it, similar to how you feel when you blend with angelic energy.

You can repeat the meditation in this chapter until you begin to sense how it feels to stay in your column and embody the divine blueprint for your life.

I don't think I'm worthy to accept my highest good.

Humans commonly have this concern. We promise that you are infinitely and undeniably WORTHY of all good. There could be no one more worthy than you. Please allow us to bring this feeling to every cell of your being.

I'm upset that I have spent so much of my life OUT of my highest good.

Many humans share this perception, and we extend our deepest compassion to you. We recommend that you pay attention to your future and what lies ahead for you, rather than to your past. See all of your experiences as important steps on your path, bringing crucial lessons you chose to learn.

Try to let go of any regrets. We understand this may be difficult, and we will assist you if you ask. There is so much more of your life and many beautiful adventures yet to come.

If you have persistent regret, we suggest that it may instead be a disguised form of resistance to moving forward.

Soul Interests

There is considerable anxiety on your planet about what is known as "life purpose." The majority of you are extremely worried about whether you have one.

We hear you saying things like the following:

- What if I don't have a life purpose?
- Am I left out?
- What is my life purpose?
- How can I find out?
- Does the universe not love me enough to give me one?
- Was I forgotten?
- I'm afraid I'll get it wrong.
- What if I fail in this lifetime?
- I might disappoint everyone.
- What if I'm just not good enough?

There is a great deal of distress about this topic. Dear reader, you have been patiently and diligently following along with this book until now. You probably can guess what we will say. Nothing that causes so much discomfort can ever benefit you.

We ask you to do what you may consider unthinkable: let go of this entire investigation and the accompanying stress!

Why? Because there is no such thing as life purpose. It does not exist.

What is likely underlying all of this anxiety about your life purpose is a fear that there is something wrong with you, you are not good enough and the universe does not love you. These are issues for you to address either in self-healing (with our help) or with a suitable professional. They have nothing to do with what is called "life purpose."

We invite you to redirect your entire spiritual experience in such a way that it is not stressful or worrisome for you at all. Please allow us to alleviate all your fear and anxiety.

Types of Soul Interests

Each incarnated human is called to certain themes and types of activities. We call them "soul interests." Your soul chose them for a particular reason, whether to learn, expand or contribute.

Soul interests are always, and without exception, positive in nature. They lovingly attract your focus and energy.

These are the four main soul interests:

1. **Connection** - helping others in any number of ways.
2. **Creative** - living and expressing the beautiful energies of creativity.

3. **Environmental** - bettering the Earth.
4. **Wisdom** - imparting knowledge and guidance, whether or not knowingly channeled.

We outline these general categories in case this helps you to assess yourself, but they are fluid in nature. Many pursuits can fit into each one. For example, a person could be called to share wisdom creatively, or to promote connection while bettering the Earth. Accordingly, a soul interest may belong to more than one category.

Identifying Your Soul Interests

How can you come to know your soul interests? We recommend that you reflect on the things you love to do. In Volume 1, we suggested you begin making decisions for your highest good according to what feels right to you (page 42). Similarly, we now propose that you make a list of what inspires and motivates you.

We encourage you to answer questions like the following:

- What interests do I love and feel passionate about?
- What activities make me happy, content, fulfilled, and satisfied when I take part in them?

- What continually captivates me, perhaps from a young age?
- What are my natural strengths?

Every human has up to three soul interests, and it is easier to pinpoint the strongest first. One soul interest will be the most dominant throughout your lifetime, taking up most of your attention and focus. But do not worry about finding it. It will find you even if you cannot locate it.

Remember to avoid being stressed about recognizing your soul interests. As we have said above, this would be completely counterproductive. We propose that you ask for angelic assistance as you explore the topic in a relaxed, curious and light-hearted way.

Life Expression Energies

So much of your human life involves the frequencies you naturally emanate and not what you DO. "Life expression" energies are what your soul chose to express in this incarnation. They radiate out of you and positively affect all those in your path.

There is absolutely no need to be anxious about identifying these energies. They will become stronger as you continue on your path, and you will effortlessly transmit them. You probably already do.

These frequencies flow from you, aiding others with what they lack in their own energy fields. This is a healing function that occurs without your conscious awareness. When you work with angels and the higher realms, it intensifies the effect.

These are the main life expression energies:

- Peace
- Harmony
- Happiness
- Joy
- Flow
- Creativity
- Empowerment
- Connection to the Divine
- Truth

When you are truly in alignment, you emit, instinctively and easily, all of these energies at once. You will also radiate the highest energy of all, that of LOVE (see Chapter 3, Love).

This is a beautiful state.

Until then, there will be one or two energies that come more naturally to you. These are your signature energies. They are the gift you offer to the Earth.

Identifying Your Life Expression Energies

Life expression energies can be uncovered by looking at patterns in your life. A strong energy tends to be felt so intensely that it inspires those around you. It can be traced through different contexts along your timeline. You may be so used to it, however, that you never noticed it before.

Ask yourself the following questions:

- Do you tend to have an inner sense of peace and harmony, even in the face of conflict?

  Then your energies would be PEACE and HARMONY (which are different but related).

- Are you usually happy, uplifting those surrounding you with your joyful state?

  Then your energies would be HAPPINESS and JOY.

- Do you flow through your life easily, encouraging your circle to do the same?

  Then your energy would be FLOW.

- Are you drawn to creative solutions, ideas and projects, inspiring others?

  Then your energy would be CREATIVITY.

- Do you tend to remind people of their inner strength and routinely assert your own?

Then your energy would be EMPOWER-MENT.

- Are you especially connected to the Divine and, because of this, those around you place more trust in the universe?

  Then your energy would be CONNEC-TION TO THE DIVINE.

- Would you say you are committed to the truth, thereby encouraging others to stand in their own truths?

  Then your energy would be TRUTH.

Introspection will allow you to see yourself in a new light and lead to more self-awareness.

The Shadow Side of Life Expression Energies

It is worthwhile to find the life expression energies you are still learning to embody. Then you can allow us to help you heal any issues preventing you from expressing them. We recommend addressing one energy at a time.

If you choose to do this, your life will gradually improve. You will feel more balanced and have a higher vibration when you are able to emit, naturally, all the life expression energies at once.

To identify the energies you have yet to master, ask yourself the following questions:

- Do you tend to experience conflict, and is this a very familiar state for you?

  Then you might be learning the energies of PEACE and HARMONY.

- Have you always struggled to be happy and find joy in things?

  Then you might be learning the energies of HAPPINESS and JOY.

- Do things not usually work out for you? Do you often have to try extremely hard to make any progress?

  Then you might be learning the energy of FLOW.

- Do you long to be creative but can't seem to express yourself?

  Then you might be learning the energy of CREATIVITY.

- Have you experienced repeated situations in your life that made you feel powerless?

  Then you might be learning the energy of EMPOWERMENT.

- Are you drawn to work with the spiritual realms, but can't quite seem to access them?

  Then you might be learning the energy of CONNECTION TO THE DIVINE.

- Do you often experience deceptions and people lying to you?

  Then you might be learning the energy of TRUTH.

We can support you in mastering these and thereby bettering your life, if you so wish.

CHAPTER 3
The Most Important Ascension Energies

DISCERNMENT

DEAREST READER, IF we were to sum up your current phase of ascension in one word, it would be "discernment." Of course, your path is exceedingly more complex than this one word, but we wish to stress its importance.

"Discernment" is the ability to make choices that are in agreement with your Higher Self, the spiritual realms and your highest good. All of these are one and the same.

Every decision you make takes you closer or further away from alignment. We discussed ALIGN-MENT in Volume 1, describing it as a feeling of things being "right." You can even sense it in your physical body (pages 42-43).

We defined it in the Glossary of Terms as follows:

> The process whereby a human being aligns his or her energy with the Divine, causing a state of great peace and relaxation. There are techniques for achieving this beautiful state and regular practice is recommended (page 65).

Now we will add, because you are ready to hear it, that DISCERNMENT is an indispensable component of alignment. Without it, you cannot become or stay aligned.

When you are fully awakened, every decision you make is a team effort. You are not the only one in charge of your life. Imagine you are flying a plane, and you have a co-pilot (several, in fact). You are guiding the direction of the plane, but your co-pilot also plays a critical role in flying. You are never alone.

Sometimes you will choose quickly, from a place of rapid intuition. This approach is perfect. You need not always take a long time to deliberate before acting.

These decisions may end up being out of alignment. You can tell by whether or not the results are peaceful and harmonious. If they are indeed misaligned, do not worry. This is normal. We invite you to work further with us to increase your connection and intuition.

Before taking larger actions that may significantly impact your life, we suggest you ask for our guidance and try to receive it. We know it can be difficult to perceive our input, especially at the beginning.

Once you are fairly sure that you have sensed our advice, we suggest that you consider following it. Of course, this is up to you. You are always free to make your own choices.

We dearly and, without exception, wish for your highest good. We never seek to control or influence you in any way. We have no motivation other than LOVE.

You are not required to come only to us. You can ask the angelic realms, the highest light, the Divine, the ONENESS. All that matters is that you consult the forces that intend for your highest benefit and good above all else.

How to Sense Guidance

This book is not focused on methods for spiritual communication.

Nonetheless, you can try the following:

- Listen to a guided meditation, or meditate on your own, if you feel able.

- Imagine you are open to answers and sit quietly, perhaps with some relaxing music.
- Mentally ask us your question and then carry on with the other activities of your day. See if you get an answer without trying. It might help to go for a mindful walk in nature.

Above all, pay attention to how you FEEL about your potential action. The more aligned option should feel light and inspired. For more on this, see Chapter 4 (Removing Outdated Frequencies & Programming).

It is always a good idea to take your time when making major decisions. Often, our input on the best choice for you becomes obvious with time.

Common Questions
How do I know if I made the right decision for myself?

Misaligned decisions usually end up in chaos, drama or some sort of lower energy. When you make aligned choices, the results will be beneficial for all. There will be pervading feelings of peace, flow and harmony. It will just feel "right."

Often, the benefits of such a decision are wider-reaching than you might think. All your choices have a greater impact than you know. This is no cause for alarm. It simply means you are much more a part of the ONENESS than you might have imagined.

Angels have a beautiful way of taking the simplest of decisions and reaching so many. We love to share BEAUTY, LOVE and HAPPINESS.

This process feels like a burden. How can I get used to it?

There is no need to do anything that feels onerous or stressful. That would defeat the purpose.

Working with the spiritual realms in this capacity becomes extremely natural if you practice it regularly. Also, you will see for yourself that the joyous benefits far outweigh any perceived burden.

As always, you have complete and sacred free will to ignore our advice at any time.

What if a decision seemed so right for me, but it actually wasn't? How can I be accurate with my discernment?

Above all, we would recommend regular practice with making intuitive choices. Sometimes it can feel like guidance is coming from the spiritual realms, but it's actually just your strong preference to take a specific course of action. You will know if this is the case when you see the fruits of your choice. Aligned decisions are self-evident, as discussed above.

Remember that you are still learning. You may accidentally make decisions out of blind desire. You might not accurately sense our guidance. In any event, please try to refrain from criticizing yourself. Mastering discernment is a work in progress and does not happen instantly. We recommend going slowly, with plenty of love, compassion and patience for yourself.

Surrender

You have been struggling for so long, putting so much effort into everything. We would like to remind you of the extraordinary power of SURRENDER.

There is a cosmic "dance," one could say, between guided effort and relaxation or surrender. This is out of balance for many of you, meaning that you are making too much effort. The result is unhappiness and unrest.

Why does this equation get out of balance? Although many factors are involved, these are the main reasons for difficulty with spiritual surrendering:

- Lack of trust in the universe
- Feeling unsafe

- Believing the world is dangerous
- Unworthiness
- Sense of rejection by the universe and by the "good"
- Fear of being disappointed or let down
- Need to control
- Scarcity mindset
- Fear of the unknown
- Unhealed past trauma

We request that you sense the above words and see how they resonate in your body and energy field. Especially notice whether you believe that you can trust the universe. We assure you that the universe is as trustworthy, safe and loving as you allow it to be. In other words, it is true that you create your own reality and future. If you hold the beliefs listed above, can you see how you might have difficulty constructing a life that you love?

You undoubtedly developed these convictions as the result of difficult experiences in your life. We invite you to return to Volume 1 and follow the healing processes contained therein.

"Dark Night of the Soul"

Many of you have experienced what is commonly known as a "dark night of the soul" or a time of many things going wrong at the same time.

What happened to you during this crisis is usually whatever it took to encourage you to have a momentous breakthrough and completely surrender to the Divine.

By practicing and welcoming spiritual surrender (see meditation below), you can avoid future periods such as these. You are not required to suffer to achieve spiritual growth.

Every wayshower currently on the planet has endured at least one dark night of the soul. We know this has been deeply upsetting and painful for you.

The dark night of the soul has been a means of getting you out of your own way. Think of the ascension process as a kind of re-birth. In order to birth the brand-new you, free of traumas and past pain, the old you must die. We do not mean this in a literal sense, of course. We mean that the old you (with all the pain, stress, worry, fear, problems, and anxiety) ceases to exist during the ascension process. This has the effect of greatly reducing your ego and your need to control every aspect of your life.

If you have gone through a dark night of the soul, you may have strongly felt some or all of the following emotions:

- Hopeless
- Completely alone

- Isolated
- Unloved and unlovable
- Shame
- Devastated
- Unworthy
- Targeted and harassed, or having "bad luck"
- Not wanting to be on the planet anymore (see note below)

"3D programming" to oppose ascension can also cause the types of emotions listed above (see Chapter 4, Removing Outdated Frequencies & Programming).

If you are going through a dark night of the soul, please know that you are loved and never alone. We and thousands of other light beings are always by your side. Try to trust the process. Know that you are safe, and that all is well. The sooner you achieve spiritual surrender, the quicker you will find relief. You will start to feel better and begin to attract more loving experiences and people into your life.

If you have already been through one, please allow us to help you release any trauma or bad feelings you may still have. Try to see this time as simply being a part of your path, without judgment.

As always, please see an appropriate professional if you feel it would benefit you.

Please note that the emotion of "not wanting to be on the planet anymore" is not the same as contemplating ending your life. If you ever feel this way, please seek urgent help.

The State of Spiritual Surrender

Surrendering helps you to accept the universe's infinite wisdom that all good can and will come to you. It means letting go completely and trusting yourself, the Divine, the universe, your helpers, your highest good, and LOVE. By surrendering, you accept that you are in an interactive universe and that, truly, and, in a very real sense, **everything is working out for you.** As we explained when we discussed discernment, you are never completely in charge of your own life, even if you believe otherwise.

The effect of embracing a state of spiritual surrender is that you feel peaceful and relaxed. You will be less controlling over your life and more easily accept help from others. It takes away a lot of stress, allowing you to embrace your path and respect others' free will.

Let's say, for example, that one of your loved ones becomes ill. Of course, this news will naturally upset you. However, with the practice of spiritual surrender, you will be better able to accept that this loved one is choosing a path different from what you would prefer for him or her (see Chapter 5, Family & Friends).

It is a good idea to take the idea of spiritual surrender a step further and trust the angelic forces to help you with any healing issues you have. With our help, you will become much more comfortable with peacefully letting go of anything that is not beneficial for you.

We invite you to practice spiritual surrender in your daily life. It can be achieved by setting a simple intention in your mind. You do not need to follow a specific meditation for this, but there is one below in case it is useful for you.

Meditation for Spiritual Surrender

1. Please find a comfortable place to sit quietly, where you will not be disturbed.
2. Take some deep breaths as you start to relax.
3. Set the intention, in your mind, to connect with our energy. If you like, you can repeat our name as a mantra in your mind: "Metatron, Metatron, Metatron."
4. Imagine that the most beautiful, sparkling white light is all around you and integrating with your physical body. As we merge our energy with yours, you will start to feel a

deep sense of safety and comfort, as if you are home. You are.

5. Breathe deeply and slowly, continuing to focus on the sparkling white light.

6. Consciously surrender to the healing power of this white light.

7. Let go of any thoughts in your mind and just relax into the energy.

8. Take a few deep breaths as you continue to allow this energy to work with you.

9. Now imagine relaxing into this universal light even more deeply. If you like, you can imagine that you are on your knees bowing down, but this is not necessary.

10. Completely give in to this loving light and feel it flowing through you.

11. If any specific situations or relationships are troubling you, imagine surrendering them to this divine light.

12. Relax and breathe for a few moments.

13. Mentally thank your helpers and guides from your heart for their assistance today.

14. Now imagine that you have tree roots coming out of the bottoms of your feet and extending deep into the Earth.

15. Visualize that you are in a super strong bubble of bright white light. This is a magic bubble, and only love can enter it.

16. When you are ready, you can begin to move your physical body and come back into the room.

If you would like to follow along with a guided meditation, you can find one here -
www.kristintaylorintuitive.com/ascensionbook2
(Meditation 2, password: loveandmagic)

You may wish to practice this meditation daily for seven days, or as long as you feel guided.

Divine Grace

Once you surrender to the Divine and realize you are not solely in charge of your experience, you will feel the most delicious sense of release. It is then that DIVINE GRACE can truly enter your life.

You can experience divine grace if you embody the states of humility, surrender, sincerity, and respect for the Divine. It is a gift and not an entitlement. The power of grace permits you to access the higher energies of love, joy, happiness, and peace. It also allows for miraculous results that could not otherwise be achieved.

To call on divine grace, make a humble and sincere request from your heart. You can ask the angels to assist you with this, and we will most happily comply.

For example, if you are looking to attract a romantic partner, you could call on divine grace to help you. It is a good idea to continue to confront and resolve any relevant healing issues you may still have. The same principles apply to any situation in your life.

The following is a suggested procedure to ask for divine grace, but you are welcome to try your own variation:

Meditation to Call on Divine Grace

1. Please find a comfortable place to sit quietly, where you will not be disturbed.
2. Mentally (or out loud) call on us, the Archangel Metatron, and your angelic helpers.
3. Allow us to bring you the energies of humility, surrender, sincerity, and respect for the Divine. Feel the sacredness of this request as you embody these, one by one.
4. From your heart and in a sincere, prayer-like fashion, make your request to the universe for divine grace. For example, you could say something like:

   "I request the intervention of divine grace

for this situation: [describe situation].
Thank you."

5. Feel the peace that follows your request.
   Breathe deeply and slowly.
6. Know that you have been heard and respect-
   fully let it all go.
7. Mentally thank your helpers and guides from
   your heart for their assistance today.

You can find a guided meditation
for this process here -
www.kristintaylorintuitive.com/ascensionbook2
(Meditation 3, password: loveandmagic)

Normally it is sufficient to ask once for each situation, but you can repeat the process if you wish.

Your request does not interfere with any efforts
you take to heal the situation by other means. We
advise you to continue with these if you so wish.

LOVE

When we asked you to take this "ride" with us,
we had a specific outcome in mind. The ultimate
goal of ascension is to radiate love from every cell
of your being and also to "ingest" it at the same
time. It is truly the highest state of consciousness.

Love is the most fundamental substance of the

universe. You could say that everything in existence is made from love, and you would be correct.

There has been a miscommunication on an enormous scale: that you are or have ever been "separate" from love. It is simply not possible. Nothing you could do or be could ever cause you to be unworthy of receiving the most essential and beautiful energy in the universe. Nothing. Everyone, without exception, deserves love.

The good news is that it is readily available all around you. If you have not been feeling this, then it is due to imbalances within you and not with a lack of supply. There is more than enough love to go around. There always has been and always will be.

When you connect to the true energy of love and are able to receive it without any obstacles or limitations, your reality completely changes. You will see the world as a more beautiful place. The trees and flowers start to sing in your presence as you notice their loving natures and brilliant colors. Life comes alive to you. Conflict will not exist nearly as much for you, and all will flow more smoothly.

There is nothing to lose and everything to gain when you connect to the true essence of love. You were not ready before this moment, but we invite you to take this journey with us now.

Meditation to Radiate Love

1. Please find a comfortable place to sit quietly, where you will not be disturbed.

2. Take some deep breaths as you start to relax.

3. Set the intention, in your mind, to connect with our energy. If you like, you can repeat our name as a mantra in your mind: "Metatron, Metatron, Metatron."

4. Imagine that the most beautiful, sparkling white light is all around you and integrating with your physical body.

5. As we merge our energy with yours, you will start to feel a deep sense of safety and comfort. Focus on these feelings.

6. Breathe deeply as you surrender to the energy working with you.

7. Bring your attention to your heart center in the middle of your chest.

8. Imagine allowing the white light to enter your heart. See your heart as being completely full of this loving white light.

9. Surrender to the healing power of this light. Let go of any thoughts in your mind and just relax into the energy.

10. Take a few deep breaths, with your sole focus on the light in the center of your chest.

11. When your heart feels very full of this healing

light, imagine that it starts to radiate out from your heart far into the universe. Remember that the more loving energy you send out, the more you receive, for there is no shortage of love.

12. Take some more deep breaths and continue to radiate light from your heart.

13. Now visualize that every cell of your body is sending love far out into the universe.

14. Notice how wonderful this feels in your body and your energy field.

15. Mentally thank your helpers and guides from your heart for their assistance today.

16. Now imagine that you have tree roots coming out of the bottoms of your feet and extending deep into the Earth.

17. Visualize that you are in a super strong bubble of bright white light. This is a magic bubble, and only love can enter it.

18. When you are ready, you can begin to move your physical body and come back into the room.

You will find a guided meditation here -
www.kristintaylorintuitive.com/ascensionbook2
(Meditation 4, password: loveandmagic)

You may wish to listen to this meditation daily

for seven days, or as long as you feel it is beneficial for you.

This is a very good practice for anyone seeking a romantic partner. It is also useful for those who wish to experience more love in their lives, generally.

The ascension path brings you out of lower-vibration energies, such as fear, hate, and envy. It takes you to the state of pure love, the highest energy you can embody.

Notice how your life changes once you receive and radiate the frequency of pure love. Your happiness levels will surely increase, and all of life will be more enjoyable for you.

We congratulate you on this important step in your ascension process.

You can "renew" your connection with love (or with the angelic realm, as this has the same effect) if you begin to feel disconnected from it at any time. Remember that any such feeling is not real, and we suggest that you take measures to realign yourself to the frequency of love as soon as you can.

CHAPTER 4
Old Planetary Energies

REMOVING OUTDATED FREQUENCIES &
PROGRAMMING

LIGHTER VIBRATIONS ARE strengthening on Earth, and what you could call the "old guard" is dissolving. Sometimes referred to as "3D" or third-dimensional energies, they are remnants of how things used to be and do not allow for all the possibilities for human potential at present.

As the planet lifts, humans are finding it harder to tolerate such dense frequencies. In the past, they could generally be around them, up to a certain level. Now, your energy systems have much higher vibrations and cannot endure as much exposure.

Yet, these frequencies are ingrained into how you habitually live your life. This means that, without your conscious awareness, the decisions you make and the company you keep may be detrimental to your wellbeing.

It can take some time to remove the outdated energies. It is important to continue and to not give up.

Choosing Lighter Energies

Many times, we are asked, "Archangel Metatron, how do we release 3D energies from our lives?"

The simple answer every time is to FEEL. Incompatible 3D density feels heavy and burdensome. You naturally tend to avoid its presence, whether this is in the form of a person, situation, workplace, television show, or anything else. The more sensitive you are, the more obvious this will be.

Higher compatible frequencies can be easily accepted into your own ascending energy system.

The major energies of ascension are:

- Peace
- Love
- Harmony
- Happiness
- Flow

They can be further described as one or more of the following:

- Light
- Loving
- Uplifting
- Expansive
- Happy
- Free
- Delightful
- Joyful
- Beneficial
- Whole

These make you feel more like who you are, in the very best expression of yourself.

Heavy energies are the opposite. They are draining, and you do not wish to experience more of them. They can give you a kind of "hangover," in that you may continue to sense them long after your initial exposure.

At this stage of your spiritual development, the difference in compatible and incompatible energies will probably be stark and easy to spot. Also, your resistance to making beneficial changes should be lessening by now. All the excuses you previously gave yourself for staying in unpleasant situations, such as "she's an old friend," or "they need me," are increasingly less important, if they come up at all.

There is no time like the present for making positive changes and for letting go of any relationships and situations that are no longer good for you. In Volume 1, we suggested that you do an inventory of everything in your life that is not adding to your happiness at least most of the time (page 44). In other words, all that is not creating in you any of the beautiful energies listed above. This is an important exercise to repeat from time to time.

The meditation below is an easy and painless way to let go, without even necessarily being aware of what is leaving you.

Bubble of White Light Meditation to Release Dense Energies

1. Please find a comfortable place to sit quietly, where you will not be disturbed.
2. Take some deep breaths as you start to relax.
3. Visualize being surrounded by the most beautiful white light. It is forming a very strong bubble around you. This is a very special bubble that only allows love and the highest frequencies to enter.
4. See all dense energies that are not compatible with this bubble floating away. These could be from relationships, situations or places. It does not matter where they originate.

5. Take some deep breaths while you continue to see all the heavy energies floating away from you.

6. Again, feel the bubble of loving white light all around you. Notice how strong it is, and how it feels comforting, safe and protective.

7. Focus on allowing even more of the dense energies to leave your space. You may sense them as they are leaving, but there is no need to try to identify them. Simply keep focusing on the beautiful bubble of light all around you.

8. When you feel that all the lower vibrations have left, return your full attention to the bubble of light. Notice its loving presence, like a warm, comforting blanket.

9. Take a few breaths, calmly and peacefully.

10. Mentally thank your helpers and guides from your heart for their assistance today.

11. Now imagine that you have tree roots coming out of the bottoms of your feet and extending deep into the Earth.

12. Notice how you are still in a super strong and protective bubble of white light.

13. When you are ready, you can begin to move your physical body and come back into the room.

You will find a guided meditation here -
www.kristintaylorintuitive.com/ascensionbook2
(Meditation 5, password: loveandmagic)

You can repeat this meditation as often as you wish. If you seek to make many changes in your life and feel encumbered by lower energies, we recommend that you listen to it more often, even daily.

"3D" Programming

All humans have been "programmed" to resist ascension and remain part of the old planetary energies. This is a fact.

You have an absolute right to choose differently, and you are doing so by reading this book.

It is important to be aware that certain emotions may come up as you shift into higher consciousness. They may appear to be warnings, but they are just part of the outdated programming.

You could experience intense fear during some or all of the ascension process. You might have an overall sense that upgrading your energy is very wrong, extremely dangerous, scary, and not allowed.

More specifically, you could find that you subconsciously hold some or all of these beliefs:

- It's so wrong to release the old energies.

- I'm not allowed to do it.
- I can't think differently than the masses.
- I'll get into terrible trouble.
- My loved ones will pay the price for this.
- Something absolutely horrible will happen if I do this.
- It's forbidden.
- I risk death if I do it.
- I could cause my family to die if I do it.
- They (your family, the world) will never forgive me if I do it.
- I'll be a freak, and I'll never fit in again.
- I'll be abused and tortured if I do it.
- Something unspeakably terrible will happen to me if I get ahead of the others.
- I'll betray them if I leave them behind.
- It's too scary to go into the unknown.
- Change isn't allowed.
- We all have to suffer together.
- I'll be all alone if I do this.
- The lower energies (including fear) are good for me and keep me safe.

Having these emotions is part of the human experience, but it is your choice whether to keep them. We can help you release them, if you so wish.

This programming accessed you through what is called mass consciousness or cultural conditioning. Perceived as the unspoken "truth," it is quietly woven into the fabric of many of your television shows, films, news programs, books, and collectively held opinions.

To resolve this issue, we recommend that you ask for our assistance and also begin to question that which you perhaps once accepted as fact. We will help you think more independently (see also Chapter 3, Discernment). The programming, which was never really yours in the first place, will start to dissolve. You will begin to sense the TRUTH.

The *Bubble of White Light Meditation*, above, or any work with us (most effectively in the form of meditation or quiet contemplation), can remove 3D programming. Please be aware that it may be deeply embedded and so could take some time to clear. This is perfectly normal and to be expected. It is a work in progress for all of you until you truly begin to be free of these influences. In the next section, and indeed throughout the course of this book, we will guide you through this transitional period.

We applaud you for your efforts, and, in time, all on your planet will be in the higher frequencies. There will be no more sources of 3D programming. Until then, it is a good idea to be sensible, practice discernment, and maintain your intellectual and energetic sovereignty.

Some of you ask why this programming exists. Our answer is that it matters not. It is not productive to consider such questions. We recommend that you look after yourself and your own energetic integrity. Focus on your own experience, which is getting happier and lighter all the time, and thereby benefiting the planet as a whole.

ENTERTAINMENT, ARTWORK & BOOKS

Dense vibrations are present in certain types of entertainment, such as music, magazines, books, television shows, and films. As we previously mentioned, this is one way that lower frequencies can be transmitted to you, without your conscious awareness.

We are in no way being judgmental. We simply wish you to be aware that certain materials contribute to the lightening of the Earth's energy, while others increase energies like violence, struggle and despair. Heavy frequencies also temporarily damage your energy systems, so we also wish to guide you, in a loving manner, on your entertainment choices.

Energy is inextricably involved in any endeavor, including creative ventures, for it is integral to everything on the planet. Some, who are already wise to how the universe works, draw on the highest light for creating their works. Their final pieces are uplifting and energetically aligned with the ascension path, in other words, with the Earth becoming more whole and joyful.

Most humans, however, do not yet know how to create from the highest universal energies. They are unaware of the energetic sources of their work. Often, they subconsciously draw from their own unhealed emotional issues. These creators also may unknowingly be the conduit of lower 3D energies. In the end, their final pieces are embedded with these vibrations.

Selecting Entertainment Sources

We recommend using discernment when choosing what to watch, read or hear.

Entertainment can be categorized as follows:

- Heavy (harmful to sensitive people)
- Uplifting or beneficial
- Harmless or neutral.

For instance, if the work largely focuses on lower energies like struggle and despair, without hope, it would belong to the old 3D frequencies (and to the "heavy" category). If the overall effect of it is inspirational, even perhaps in the face of challenges, then it would fit into the "uplifting" category. If it is generally positive, but also with a fair amount of lower energies, it would probably be "harmless."

We realize that you may not always know in advance whether something you watch or read is positive for you. In time, you will be able to use your intuition to sense what is harmless, if not beneficial, for you. We recommend simply doing your best, without stress or anxiety.

It is always your sacred right to select entertainment and everything else in your life. These are simply our recommendations, given with the sole intention to help you feel increasingly better.

Avoiding Entertainment with Heavy Energies

Heavy sources of entertainment are those which are low-vibration and bring you down. Indications of this would be if the work contains a great deal of violence, despair, lack of safety, fear, poverty, illness, or similar energies. Overall, it has a harsh and dismal tone. There are no positive transformations in it and not many, if any, light energies such as hope, happiness or kindness.

However, you cannot always depend on these criteria. Sometimes a piece can have a not-too-depressing theme and still be full of lower energies. Another show with a similar storyline could be harmless to watch. In the first example, the dense frequencies have accidentally been infused into the piece by its makers.

To avoid this type of entertainment, you would have to rely exclusively on your intuition and how you feel about watching it. You can also see how you feel in your body when thinking about it and, if you get that far, when exposed to it.

As for music, you can loosely apply the same criteria. "Heavy" music feels dense, while high-er-vibration music has a lighter energy. You may find that your body can sense the difference.

We are always here to guide you and help you with your intuition, should you so wish. If you do not accurately sense if something is heavy or not beforehand, please do not worry.

We encourage you to discontinue watching, reading or listening, even mid-way through, to anything that makes you feel unwell in any way.

If you are exposed to a low-vibration entertain-ment source for longer than a brief period, you may not feel like yourself afterwards. This is temporary, and please do not blame yourself in any way. You are learning what is best for you within the context of the new planetary energies. We recommend that you work with us so we can clear your energy field and restore your frequency. One way to do this would be to follow the *Shower of Light Meditation* in Chapter 6 (Maintaining Your Energy Integrity).

We do not mean to say that you can never enjoy entertainment, or that you have to be so careful to the point it is burdensome. Of course, you are free to choose whatever you wish. You can use your ever-increasing skill of discernment, and we fully encourage this. Your experience will help guide your future decisions.

Identifying Uplifting Entertainment

Some types of entertainment are beneficial in that you feel better after watching, reading or listening to them. You can use your intuition to determine the general feeling of the piece to see if it is uplifting.

For anything with a storyline, you might also like to ask these questions before you decide whether to consume it:

- Do the characters feel they live in a fundamentally safe universe, or do they begin to feel this way?
- Even if they have difficulties, are they empowered or start to be?
- If any misconceptions like scarcity, lack or fear are present in the piece, are they corrected by the end?

- Is the overall effect to uplift or inspire the audience?

Remember that the Earth is moving into a phase where LOVE and LIGHT will dominate. This is a beautiful and much-needed transition.

So, a final question (and perhaps the most important of all) would be:

Does this creative work belong to the new planetary energies?

You will be able to answer affirmatively to the above questions if a piece of entertainment is uplifting.

We realize that the choices available to you at this point in time will not always fit these standards. However, if you are fairly sure that something definitely does not belong to the new energetic framework, or is at least leaning in that direction, it is better to avoid it. It pays to be mindful about what you ingest into your being. We do not simply mean food and drink. We mean all forms of input and influences.

It is a time of connection, heart-centered conversation, love, and inspiration. It is no longer the time for lower energies, such as violence and despair.

Harmless or Neutral Entertainment

"Harmless" entertainment is that which sits in the middle. It has too many low energies to be considered "uplifting" and not enough to be seen as "heavy." It is somewhat positive and inspirational. You can watch, read or listen to this without receiving any benefits but also without incurring any damage to your energy system.

At this point in time, we recognize that not all entertainment you consume will elevate your vibration, because the world is still very much adjusting to the higher frequencies. As always, whether you choose to ingest these sources is up to you.

Advice for Artists & Creators

As we explained above, sometimes makers and artists accidentally transmit lower frequencies through their creations. It would be beneficial if more consideration was given to the energetic quality of entertainment and art before it is disseminated.

We understand it may be challenging for you to determine which creative works are best shared with others and which are better kept to yourself. We suggest that you use discernment, along with our guidance below. With practice, this evaluation will become easier.

We will now suggest some criteria that can help artists and creators when deciding whether to share their pieces with others.

Works that would benefit the world if they were shared:

Anything uplifting, hopeful or inspiring. It would belong to the "uplifting" category above. It brings a good feeling to the viewer or listener, and there is an ongoing ripple effect of beautiful energy every time the piece is enjoyed. Please see the previous section of this chapter for how to identify higher frequencies.

Works made for purposes of your own healing that would be best kept private:

Anything which assists you in your own healing journey. This could include the exploration and expression of distressing feelings, past abuse or trauma through the creative process. It also includes those works created as a commentary on the "painful" or "upsetting" state of the world, according to your perception.

We do not mean that entertainment can never contain "negative" topics, for these exist as part of the human experience. We request that you examine the piece (whether it is a book, artwork, film, television show, or something else) and look at the viewpoint it employs.

In addition, we are not saying that creative ventures and art cannot be used for healing, because they can. This is a worthwhile use for creativity. However, it is important to be mindful of your intentions when making something and to consider carefully how you will share it with the world. Perhaps those pieces that reflect your own healing journey would be best kept for yourself. It would be an excellent idea to discard or destroy them to help transition the energy into a more positive state.

If you wish to produce works that have a higher vibration, you would also benefit from applying to them the criteria for selecting "uplifting" entertainment, above. We would also suggest further work with us and beings of the highest light for this purpose.

We recommend that creators start producing works that are in alignment with the energies of ascension. In the near future, this will no longer be optional. The ability to transmit energy through entertainment, which has been so misused, will soon be a means to inspire and spread light.

Common Questions

I enjoy watching documentaries and biographies. Is this a good idea?

We would never advise you on what specifically you should watch. We would say it is best to apply the factors outlined above to see if this program would be beneficial or harmless for you to watch. You can also see how many (if any) of the ascension energies seem to be present in the show. You can practice using your intuition to sense this beforehand.

Even if a story is true to life, in that the events actually happened, it does not mean it is beneficial for you. If it would fit the "heavy" category, above, then watching it could damage your energy field, at least temporarily.

What about true crime? Is watching that a good idea?

Generally, what is referred to as "true crime" is very heavy in nature. We recommend using your intuition and referencing the guidance above.

I love heavy metal music. Is this damaging for me?

As you continue on your ascension path, you will be less drawn to this type of music. A song could have uplifting or empowering lyrics, but the music itself will probably be too harsh for your energy system. Your sensitivity will have increased with your spiritual development. You will eventually find that you are naturally drawn to gentler energies in everything. Positive music, whether upbeat or relaxing, will become more attractive to you. Until then, we recommend applying the guidance in this section, as well as using your intuition, to assess the general feeling of the songs.

I feel like angry music and depressing films can be healing for me. Do you not recommend them for this purpose?

There are many ways to heal and express your emotions. This is one way that can indeed be beneficial. Unfortunately, however, sometimes music and films with low vibrations can damage your energy system, as explained above. So we recommend taking a cautious approach with this. Perhaps another healing method would benefit you more. You could try journaling or working with us (see the processes in Volume 1, for example).

I find this all really difficult and burdensome. Do I really have to think about it?

You never have to do anything you do not wish to do. You always have the sacred right of free will. We would never, nor could we ever, violate that.

We invite you to try making more informed choices about entertainment and see how you feel. If it does not make a difference for you, then by all means, disregard our words.

Even if this chapter does not make sense to you now, in time it will likely become more relevant, as you continue along the ascension path.

If you feel worried or stressed about applying these principles, please feel free to ignore them. As always, we are with you every step of the way, whether or not you follow our guidance.

Attraction To Lower Energies

Many humans on your planet are interacting with harmful frequencies without realizing it. Their energy fields are infused with them, affecting decision-making and preferences in all things.

Such individuals might be naturally drawn to harshness in all forms, including heavy music, violent films and even abusive relationships. The vibration of these is quite dense, consisting, for instance, of frequencies like anger, violence, hatred, and pain. We would not call it light or uplifting, nor would anyone.

After an extended exposure, the energetic effect of such influences is profound: humans become one with them at the cellular level. With an identical point of attraction, they will then draw in even more of the same types of experiences, without their conscious awareness or understanding.

Dearest reader, we have explained to you how to identify lighter frequencies and thus avoid this situation. Yet, you may still be drawn to old 3D energies. If so, please be gentle with yourself as you transition out of it.

Strong Pull to 3D Energies

Many humans wish to make lighter choices, but find it difficult or impossible to do so. They are so subconsciously attracted to dense energies that it is like an addiction. This could affect all their preferences, including in food, entertainment, romantic partners, sexuality, and friendships. Every choice they make has pervasive lower frequencies. This may not be obvious at first, so it could come as a surprise later on.

A majority of the time, this person's life will feel like a constant struggle, with drama, "bad luck," and negative experiences. The light energies mentioned earlier in this chapter are largely absent from his or her life. The individual will find it difficult to maintain a clear energy field.

Some of you reading this book may resonate with this description to a certain extent. In this case, we encourage you to consider, with self-love and compassion, whether you have any attraction to lower energies and, if so, allow us to help you with it.

Healing an Attraction to Lower Energies

If you feel you are indeed drawn to lower frequencies, please do not blame yourself. You have done nothing wrong. It is important to forgive yourself for this and for everything.

We are happy to help you with the following, should you so wish:

- Aligning you to higher energies and removing your interest in denser vibrations.
- Identifying and resolving any underlying healing issues. For example, if you came from an abusive home, you would naturally be drawn to harsh frequencies until your experience has been fully healed.
- Overcoming any other addictions. People with an attraction to lower energies often have other addictive behavior that perpetuate their misalignment.

You may also benefit from seeing an appropriate professional.

We advise you to withdraw your attention, and, thereby, your energy, from any influence (music, film, person, relationship, place) that is heavy in nature. Workplaces and relationships do not have to be 100% positive all the time, for this is not humanly possible. Their overall feeling, however, should be light and expansive, not burdensome and draining.

When assessing a relationship or situation, ask yourself, "am I feeding from it or is it feeding off of me?" Murky energy sources, no matter how "dressed up," stylish or popular, **always feed off of you.** There is no exception. Light energies such as love, fun, joy, and happiness **always feed you.** You will soon get used to being fed by the universe instead of being a human banquet.

It can take some effort and discipline to withdraw permanently from all sources of lower frequencies. We realize that you might have to take up different hobbies or make new friends, but we assure you that the beautiful experience of ascension is worth all of this effort and more. If this is onerous for you, remember you can take small steps.

Keep in mind we are not saying that you can never watch a popular film or listen to the radio. We are not suggesting anything so extreme. We are simply proposing a new way of thinking and also recommending for you to be mindful of your selections.

The entertainment we suggest avoiding is that

which is extraordinarily harsh or violent, or which makes you feel low and heavy. We also recommend a limited period of exposure to denser energies, in whatever form, since the human body finds it easier to tolerate these influences in small doses. How long is your choice, however, we advise you to find a time limit that works for you. Please refer to the previous section in this chapter for more information.

You are always free to do whatever you wish, and this book merely offers suggestions for those who are ready and willing to listen. We never wish to control you in any way.

Common Questions
What if I have partially withdrawn from dense energies, but I still have "guilty pleasures?"

Many lightworkers and wayshowers are currently having trouble stepping up to their full paths. They still allow themselves the occasional "indulgence" in the old planetary energies. Perhaps they enjoy very harsh music or violent films. Or they drink excessively or take drugs. Or they engage in sexual relations devoid of love and with partners they hardly know. They probably sense that these things are damaging their energy fields and causing unnecessary drama and hardship in their lives. Yet, they continue to do them anyway, "compartmentalizing" their lightwork.

We must emphasize yet again that we are not judging anyone. We are merely giving you direction to help you reach the blissful state of ascension as soon as you can.

In that vein, we urge you to refrain from being a "part-time" lightworker. Interacting with 3D energies some of the time is a game that you will not win. If this is happening for you, we encourage you to examine and release your resistance to going "all-in" with your connection to the higher realms.

Ask yourself, what is causing you to hold back part of your energy in the old 3D reality?

It could be for one or more of these subconscious reasons:

1. Fear. It feels too scary for you to enter completely into the light. This could be subconscious.

2. Familiarity. You hesitate to leave the version of the world where it is "comfortable" and "safe," even if the 3D energies are making your life difficult.

3. Solidarity. You are reluctant to move forward when your family and most of the planet are still "stuck" behind. You're finding it difficult to lead the way.

4. Resistance. On some level, you are refusing

to accept the ascension energies and wishing for things to stay the same, perhaps for sentimental reasons or due to fear of change.

5. Rebellion. Ascension reminds you of being bossed around by a parental authority. So you rebel against it. Doing this makes you feel empowered and in control of your life, but these feelings are inaccurate.

6. Marketing. Some marketing makes 3D energies look stylish, fun, enticing, naughty, and captivating. You have understandably bought into this illusion. How often does the media make excessive drinking seem normal? What about casual sex? It is possible that this marketing is playing on your weaknesses, which can make avoiding low-frequency activities even more challenging for you. Do not worry, we are supporting you every step of the way.

We encourage all lightworkers and wayshowers to immerse themselves in the light and to discontinue practices they know to be fueled by lower vibrations.

If harsh frequencies, in whatever form, are still very important to you, then we ask you to consider whether you are resistant to becoming lighter. The ascension process is about letting go of the old and learning new ways to be happier than ever. The saying is true, if you do what you've always done, you'll get what you've always gotten. If you are opposed to fully adopting our suggestions, we invite you to do a trial of them to see how you feel.

Energetic Guns

We describe an energetic "gun" as anything that is so important to you that you will compromise your own energy field and wellbeing so as not to lose it. This has a very detrimental effect on you.

We tell our advanced students that they cannot have any guns to their heads. We work with them to release all their guns, and they become what the author likes to call "bulletproof." We agree with her terminology.

For example, one of our students was terrified of her husband leaving her. She would accept all kinds of behavior from him because she knew she could never leave him. What was the energetic gun to her head? Her fear of being without her husband. We worked with her to let go of this fear, and she became more balanced and detached. Her relationship with her husband vastly improved.

Another student was protective of her family members in an imbalanced way. Any issue that affected them deeply destabilized and upset her. This happened on a continual basis. What was the gun to her head? Her fear of something bad happening to any member of her family, and of them dying. She also believed that the world was an unsafe and dangerous place. We worked with her to ease her fears and help her to understand that everyone, even her family members, is on his or her own path. She was able to detach and allow them space to live their own lives. She no longer became upset by the drama that they routinely experience.

Many lightworkers allow themselves to be drained when their heart centers are activated. In other words, when they feel love or compassion for someone, they open their energy fields, usually in an effort to help or rescue the person.

World situations can hold guns to your head. Perhaps poverty doesn't trigger you, but what about garbage in the oceans? Child molestation? Cruelty to animals? Genocide? War? Rape? Pandemics? Which of the 3D energies gets you the most upset?

Sometimes an energetic gun is trendy, and so it appears to not be heavy. Usually disguised as morally right, there may be huge social pressure to support a cause. You could even be shamed by others and seen as a terrible person if you don't share in the worry and drama. We assure you that all of these tactics are merely efforts to maintain the status quo of 3D energies on the planet! Believe it or not, if you get upset by it, it is holding a gun to your head and causing you to lose your power.

You may not find out what upsets you until you are confronted with it. Even if you think you are no longer affected by it, a shock or unexpected event could prove otherwise. We suggest you make a note of your reaction and accompanying dip in vibration. Then work with us, if you like, to resolve the matter.

It is possible to help with world issues and remain energetically clear. However, if you assist out of any emotion other than love, you have an energetic gun to your head. This achieves nothing and simply aligns you with lower frequencies. You energetically unite with something, whether you support or oppose it. This is harmful to anyone who is sensitive, so please take care.

How to Work with Us to Release Energetic Guns

We encourage you to make a list of the following:

1. **Your deepest fears.** These could include being alone, your romantic partner leaving you, or losing your family. You may not be able to access all of them, but we are happy to inspire you, if you wish.

2. **Anything or anyone that "tugs at your**

heartstrings." In other words, your compassion and love for a person makes you want to rescue him or her. You may see this individual as a helpless victim, and deserving of your help. You might feel the same way about certain causes or groups, like the homeless, refugees, abused animals.

3. **All the things that deeply offend you in the world, from pollution to politics to child abuse.** This is anything that feels unfair or unjust to you. You feel a strong urge to help bring justice and "set it right."

For anything that pulls at your heartstrings, it is helpful to remember that everyone is safe and on his or her own path, even your close friends and family members. This is also true for animals. We will help balance your sense of compassion. See Chapter 5 for advice about family and friends.

With world issues, it is important to realize that we (angels and beings of the highest light) are working to improve everything. You do not have to assist anyone directly. You can do so, if you wish, but it's best if it is not out of a sense of emergency or a need to rescue.

We request that you sit with us so we can help ease your fears and remove your usual triggers. We require this work of all our advanced students.

Should you wish to proceed with us, you are no exception.

It is important to be patient with yourself while you are removing energetic guns. By following the process, in time, you can become "bulletproof" in the energetic sense.

Meditation to Release Energetic Guns

1. Please find a comfortable place to sit quietly, where you will not be disturbed.
2. Take some deep breaths as you start to relax.
3. Set the intention, in your mind, to connect with our energy. If you like, you can repeat our name as a mantra in your mind: "Metatron, Metatron, Metatron."
4. Imagine that the most beautiful, sparkling white light is all around you and integrating with your physical body. As we merge our energy with yours, you will start to feel a deep sense of safety and love.
5. Breathe slowly, focusing on the wonderful feelings we are bringing to you.
6. Bring to mind an energetic gun to your head. This could be a fear, worry or anything on your list.
7. Surrender this issue to the healing power of the white light.

8. Focus on your connection to the light as we help you to release the issue's hold over you.

9. Visualize it being immersed in the white light.

10. Breathe deeply as you allow us to ease your fears and bring you a new perspective.

11. Take a few moments to breathe slowly while you focus on the white light.

12. Now think of another energetic gun. It can be anything that compromises your energy.

13. Imagine it being immersed in white light.

14. Breathe deeply as you allow a new perspective on this issue.

15. Breathe in the energy of peace as you relax even more.

16. Mentally thank your helpers and guides for their assistance today.

17. Now imagine that you have tree roots coming out of the bottoms of your feet and extending deep into the Earth.

18. Visualize that you are in a super strong bubble of bright white light. This is a magic bubble, and only love can enter it.

19. When you are ready, you can begin to move your physical body and come back into the room.

If you prefer to listen to a guided meditation, there is one here - www.kristintaylorintuitive.com/ascensionbook2 (Meditation 6, password: loveandmagic)

You can do this meditation daily until you feel the energy becoming lighter. It is a good idea to repeat it until the issue has been completely healed. We propose that you go through this process for each major energetic gun you have identified. You can also return to it at any time.

Common Questions
I really feel the need to be an activist for a certain cause. Is this not recommended?

If you decide to support a cause, think about how you are contributing your energy. Are you participating from the vibration of love? Are you having fun and enjoying yourself while you make a difference? Or are you reacting out of anger and attacking others? We are sure you can sense which of these has the lightest vibration.

Also, consider if you **need** to be involved in this cause or if you **choose** to do so? Having a strong need to do something indicates an underlying emotional issue.

Whether you are for or against something, you are merging with it. The best protest is to ignore

75

what you are "against" and focus on what you are "for." No cause is worth sacrificing your own personal health and happiness.

I feel so drawn to politics, and my involvement in it is very important to me. Is it really best for me to change this?

We understand the draw to politics as it appears to be making the planet a better place. Each of your political parties believes it has the unique answer to help the world progress to the next level.

We do not mean to disparage the political system, for it is not all bad. It achieves some good for the human race. More will be accomplished in the future as the planet becomes lighter, with politicians more heart-centered.

What damages you is the intense and often mean-spirited combat many of you engage in with the opposite side. There is no need for this warfare, and it is of no benefit. It usually happens when being part of a certain political party becomes your identity. This is not healthy. You are a divine spark of light and always have been. Nothing can define you beyond that.

If you are angry about politics, your involvement is an energetic gun. We understand it may be difficult to see when you so vehemently oppose the other side's position. Please try to see the truth and remove this density from your life.

We know this is a sensitive topic for you, but we wish to assist you to see a higher perspective. As ever, we are here to help you with everything, in every way.

It is possible to participate in politics from an elevated frequency. Again, look at the manner in which you are taking part. Is it from an aggressive, hostile place which is typical of traditional politics? Or is it from a loving, cooperative, heart-centered approach, more in alignment with your role as a lightworker? If it is the latter, then your participation will be beneficial for you and for all involved.

It should be noted that the current political climate, at the time of writing this book, is not as receptive to lightworkers in public office as it will be in the future.

I am dedicated to doing my part to take care of the environment. Is this harmful to my vibration?

It makes a huge difference whether you are taking steps to look after the Earth in a loving and calm way, as you would care for someone you deeply love, or if you are enraged and militant in your efforts. It also matters if you are compassionate and kind to yourself and others, or critical, as you take steps to care for the planet.

Always look to the energy behind, and therefore attached to, your efforts, for it is much more important than the actions themselves. We would say that the attached energy is actually the PRIMARY energy, and it is the only one that truly matters.

So, we say, yes, it is a beautiful idea to look after the Earth in sustainable ways, such as recycling and reducing waste. Yet, the primary energy behind your endeavors must always be love or there is no point in carrying out your activities. If you did so, you would be spreading dense frequencies, which would be truly counterproductive to what you intended.

Everything you do must be undertaken with the highest and most loving intentions (and therefore, energies), or else we would counsel you to refrain from it. Similarly, if there is something you would like to partake in, but the idea of it causes you great distress, we would suggest that you not do it.

In the not-so-distant future, the products you purchase and your way of life will be complementary, rather than harmful, to your planet. This is part of the Great Awakening, or ascension, as it has been called. Until then, we suggest you focus on taking measures to raise your own energetic vibration, as outlined in this book and in Volume 1 of this series. When enough of you have made these crucial energetic changes, the planetary shifts will occur beautifully and naturally.

I have so many energetic guns to my head. How will I ever clear them all?

We sympathize with your situation, and we understand this is challenging for you. We recommend that you to take one step at a time, working to clear your most powerful energetic guns first. We will be helping you to change your perspective so that you do not continue to collect guns from this point forward. We suggest that you persevere and continue clearing, for you will surely feel better the more you release.

Also, it is perfectly fine to take a break if you need one. Go at your own pace. There is never a reason to feel pressured, stressed or worried about any of our work together, and we certainly do not wish this for you.

How can I best get through a pandemic or world disaster?

We invite you to see everything, including pandemics and any other disasters, as potential energetic guns. If this is the case, let them go in the usual way by using the *Meditation to Release Energetic Guns,* found earlier in this section.

We also advise you to let go of fear at all levels of your being. Your experience during a world crisis, and indeed at all times, is directly related to the level of fear in your energy field. Please refer to the *Meditation to Dissolve Fear* in Chapter 6 (Maintaining Your Energy Integrity).

We realize that many of you in this situation will have experienced a significant reduction in your financial livelihoods. You may also be very concerned about your health. Yet, the frequencies of abundance and wellbeing are still very much present for you. The angelic forces can show you the truth about this.

As always, we invite you to create your own reality.

You are never alone, and you are never helpless or without options. We are always, and without exception, here to assist you with all of your needs and desires.

It may be beneficial to control your exposure to the news media and fearful individuals. Please review our guidance on this in the previous section and in Chapter 5 (Family & Friends).

CHAPTER 5
Family, Relationships & Sexuality

FAMILY & FRIENDS

EVERYONE ON THE planet has a different level of vibration. You are forging ahead with lightening yours, which means you may find that you feel less dynamic in the company of some of your loved ones.

Being around, especially for an extended period, a person who is too immersed in 3D energies will reduce your frequency. This could cause you to experience, on a temporary basis, dense energies, such as fear, doubt and conflict, without understanding why. It will also reduce your vitality.

You will find that the effect on you will vary according to the other person's energetic level. In other words, it will depend on whether he or she is lower in vibration than yourself, extremely resistant to ascension, or somewhere along the continuum.

This could lead you to make some changes. You will probably wish to make lighter, higher-vibration friends, who feel good to be around and are more in line with your own rising frequency. You may decide to keep your old friends and still see your lower-vibration family members, but you will probably start to manage your interactions with them in a different way. You may choose to avoid, as much as possible, or end relationships with any friends and family members who are very opposed to ascension.

Of course, this is all up to you.

We can assist you with your decision-making, becoming more independent and having stronger energetic boundaries, if you wish.

This section provides our guidance on the matter, which you can accept or reject according to your divinely given free will.

We are sharing this information for your general awareness. We are not explaining it to be critical of anyone, in any way.

Understanding Energetic Vibration

We have spoken to you a great deal in this book about "vibration" and "frequency." But what do those terms mean, you might ask?

A person's energetic vibration can be seen as ranging from very low to very high, and anywhere in between.

Some indications of a low vibration would be, for example, if the person:

- Has not begun or just started his or her healing journey.
- Is in the middle of processing past issues.
- Has endured a great deal of abuse, and it is largely unresolved.
- Has addictions or very unhealthy habits.
- Is resistant to the ascension process, for whatever reason (see below).

Any one of the above factors could lead to a low frequency.

You, on the other hand, are raising your vibration and moving fast on your ascension path. It would unquestionably be more enjoyable for you to spend time with others who are like-minded.

If you choose to spend time with anyone who currently has a low vibration, those on the higher end of the scale are easier for you to be around than those at the lower end.

How can you tell someone's approximate level, you might ask? We will start by describing those who are very resistant to ascension, because they are the most straightforward to identify.

Those Resisting Ascension

You may have noticed that some of your family and friends are very resistant to the ascension process. Irrespective of age, many humans are defending their usual habits and ways of interacting. They subconsciously want the familiar to stay in place, even if it is harmful to them and others. So, there is often a clash between those who embrace the new, uplifting energies and those who remain loyal to "tradition."

Any of your loved ones strongly wishing to stay in the 3D reality will feel threatened, on some level, by your rising vibration. They will want you to stop improving yourself and disrupting the status quo. Without their conscious awareness, they will try to hold you back from your ascension process. Accordingly, you may seem to "backtrack" when you are with them. We are not judging your loved ones, or anyone else, but merely wish to bring your attention to this matter.

How to Tell if Someone is Resisting Ascension

If your loved one is strongly opposing ascension, you will probably feel ill or less energetic around them. You might have a low mood during or after seeing them. It is also possible you may find yourself hiding your spiritual progress from them because they seem closed off to change, and especially to positive transformation.

This person will seek to introduce lower energies into their conversations and interactions. They will try to redirect conversations to that effect, extending them as long as possible. Of course, this is all beyond their conscious awareness.

These are signs of being subconsciously against ascension:

- They are "stuck in their ways" and oppose new ideas.
- Their moods are often low, and they experience little joy. A common pattern is to blame this on family members, relationships or world events.
- They wish to discuss, at length, distressing personal issues. They may say they want your advice, but the conversation nonetheless does not get any lighter. They typically do not find solutions to their problems because they are not open to them.

- Their projects and plans never seem to work out, giving them more fuel for their discussions.
- They reminisce about the "good old days" and believe the world is getting much worse.
- They seem to be very troubled by world affairs, politics and injustices, such as homelessness or poverty. This may be confusing for you, because they can appear to be really compassionate and caring about these matters. However, this is just another reason to engage in low-frequency conversations.
- They watch or listen to a great deal of news programs (especially if they are unsettling or shocking) and recite back the information, seeking to go over it with you at length.
- They enjoy violent, low-vibration television programs, films and other kinds of heavy entertainment.
- They may crave sexual relationships that are purely physical in nature.

These characteristics are symptomatic of the old 3D energy, although a resistant person may not display them all at once.

This is not your loved one's fault, and we are not blaming him or her in any way. If he or she is making progress towards ascension, even if slow, then some areas will show signs of improvement.

Remind yourself that your loved ones are on their own paths and moving at their own pace.

Why People Oppose Ascension

Most people object to ascension because they fear anything new. They are very familiar with their old patterns, and they want to keep them. It is proven in your current science that the human brain resists the unknown.

Another reason is that the masses still do not wish to change. This is slowly shifting. However, many humans do not want to stand out against the crowd, because this would make them feel unsafe and like they do not fit in with others.

So, we applaud you, dear reader, for taking the leap into ascension. We know how much courage this has taken, and we congratulate you. Your efforts are seen and celebrated by us.

The Effect of Being Around Those Resisting Ascension

When others oppose ascension, it directly affects you when you are in their presence, whether in person or via the telephone. It can indeed be tough to be in their company while you are progressing with your own self-development. This is true whether or not they are family members. It is difficult because you take a step forward, and then it feels as if they have pulled you back.

Sensitive people often report feeling drained after having spent significant time around others with very low vibrations. There is much discussion about ways to protect and manage your energy. We simply recommend staying away from such people as much as possible, and certainly until you are further along in your own ascension process. We understand that this may be challenging for you to accept.

If you cannot avoid them completely, we recommend trying to be with them as infrequently as possible and avoiding any personal conversations. Spending too much time with resistant people, even if they are your loved ones, hampers your spiritual growth and is detrimental to your energy system. When you feel drained or ill, you know you have been in their company too long.

We do not advise you to discuss low-vibration, heavy topics at length with anyone. Such conversations have a direct, harmful effect on your body and energy field. You are a sensitive person, and you cannot be around large amounts of dense energy. Your body can no longer process it because you are not entirely part of the old planetary frequency anymore. In fact, no one's energy system can process it, which is why (in part) so much illness and unhappiness exists in the 3D world.

If you wish to spend time with someone who is strongly opposing ascension, you might like to ask yourself the following questions:

- Why do I feel the need to be around this friend or family member?
- What hidden benefit is being in his or her company providing to me?
- Is this relationship (or my loyalty to it) an energetic gun? Please see Chapter 4 (Energetic Guns).
- Am I not trusting the ascension process fully?
- Does part of me want to stay in the old planetary energies where it is familiar?
- Am I accepting feeling less than my best around this person for some reason, like needing to please them?

By avoiding very low-vibration friends and family, or limiting your exposure to them, you are not losing them. You are simply giving them and yourself the space you each need to develop and grow at your own pace.

You can try to use energy-management techniques for your visits with them. Please keep in mind that sometimes these methods will not be effective, especially if you have used them for a while.

It is our general recommendation that you embrace energetically lighter new friends. If you feel able, we suggest that you avoid, or take steps to remove, in a loving manner, extremely resistant people from your life. We realize that this may be more challenging for you when it comes to family members.

We do not recommend that you live with anyone who is extremely resistant to ascension. This situation will be very difficult for you. If it does not improve in time, we suggest that you transition out of it as soon as you are able.

If you wish to change your living arrangements, we will assist you with this. We will inspire you with practical steps and guidance. Please try to release any fear you might have and take small steps if you can. You may wish to listen to the *Meditation to Dissolve Fear* in Chapter 6 (Maintaining Your Energy Integrity).

You may feel a sense of duty to be around all your friends and family members, regardless of their energetic state. We understand this, and we would never suggest that you neglect or abandon anyone. Again, consider whether this well-intentioned feeling is actually an energetic gun (see Chapter 4, Energetic Guns). In any event, our guidance is given with love, but you are always free to make your own choices.

We are not asking you to love those close to you any less. We are advising that you spend less time with anyone when doing so would have an adverse effect on your energy system.

Those with Low Vibrations

Some people have low vibrations, even if they are not opposing ascension. They have chosen, at a higher level, to upgrade their energy fields, but they are going slowly. They may mildly fit the criteria above (for identifying resistant people), or they may not. In any case, you will be able to gauge their level of vibration by how you feel around them. You will also get a sense of this by their preferences and topics of conversation: whether they are generally light or heavy.

Everyone is free to raise his or her vibration at any time, according to free will. For example, a friend could be inspired by your healing journey and decide to begin one, too. This would probably make it easier for you to be in his or her company. However, it is important to never pressure your loved ones to go more quickly than they desire.

Spending Time with a Low-Vibration Person

The further along in your ascension journey, the more likely you are to encounter those with a lower energy frequency than your own. This is unavoidable.

We do not expect you to remove everyone from your life, nor would we advise that.

If you wish to see others who have a low vibration, we would suggest the following:

- Allow us to help you with the situation and also with establishing energetic boundaries.
- Employ the energy management techniques provided in Chapter 6 (Maintaining Your Energy Integrity). You may wish to do so before and after your visit with the person.
- Limit the amount of time you spend with him or her.

Whatever you choose, we suggest that you find a way to avoid your vibration dropping, if at all possible. You will discover, through trial and error, what works best for you.

As a reminder, it is universal law that if you are around energies that are lower than yours for some time, you will undoubtedly be affected. It is vital to cleanse your energy if you feel that it has been compromised. You will know this is the case if you feel down or not like yourself. This could happen after spending time with anyone with a lower vibration than your own.

You are learning to control your energy field. Once you have stabilized it and feel more firmly aligned with the higher frequencies, it may be possible to be with low-vibration family and friends for longer periods with fewer harmful effects, if any, and less need for energy-management methods. However, you may find that you no longer wish to do so.

Living with a Low-Vibration Person

This is a challenging situation and can be exhausting for you.

Here are some strategies:

- Focus on yourself and your self-care as much as possible.
- Remember to work with angels daily in meditation.
- Release your own resistance to letting this person leave your life if it is for your highest good.
- Become very proficient at energy management techniques, and do them regularly (see Chapter 6, Maintaining Your Energy Integrity).
- Continue with your own healing journey.

You may wish to ask specifically for angelic help with the following:

- Shifting the situation in the best way for both of you.
- Giving you their higher perspective of the situation.
- Holding your energy at all times and acting as a buffer between you and the person.

Above all, we recommend continuing with your own healing journey. Sometimes it is easier to focus on others instead of confronting your own issues. You could find that, as you continue along your healing journey, your relationship automatically becomes easier. This is not always the case, however. Perhaps it is a good idea to give yourself a time limit for how long you will stay in the situation.

If it does not improve after some time, and you are finding it difficult to maintain your energy level in the company of this person, we lovingly suggest that you find a new living arrangement. We do not recommend that you suffer in any way, including when you cohabitate with others.

Transitioning Out of Friendships & Relationships

In most cases, a physical separation will happen naturally after you set the intention to receive only high-frequency, light individuals into your personal life. You and your former friend will usually grow apart, without any effort on your part. This is due to your increasing difference in vibration, which naturally creates a sense of distance between you.

Sometimes others may not wish to leave your life, even if you desire for them to do so. In this case, we nonetheless advise you to follow what is best for you. It is your choice as to who is in your private life. We are here to help you, as always.

Once you have separated physically from the person, there is always an energetic tie that remains. If you wish, we can assist you by removing this from your energy field.

Identifying Higher-Vibration People

You will find it fairly easy to spot individuals with higher frequencies.

You may find that they:

- Are on a spiritual path that has an uplifting and expansive quality to it.
- Have embraced their healing journeys.

- Seem to embody at least some of the ascension energies, to a greater or lesser extent (see Chapter 4, Removing Outdated Frequencies & Programming).
- Engage in conversations about energetically light topics.
- Avoid gossiping about others.
- Enjoy themselves and have fun.
- Tend to see possibilities rather than limits.
- Are happy, for the most part, even if things are not perfect.
- Continue to improve themselves, usually by a variety of means.
- Are generally compassionate and loving.
- Seem to radiate high-frequency energies like love and peace.

Overall, you feel good around them and tend to feel happier after having been with them. Please also refer to the list of light feelings in Chapter 4 (Removing Outdated Frequencies & Programming).

This is just a guideline. A high-vibration person might not fit all the criteria, and may meet some more than others.

Everyone has moments when they have lower vibrations, even those who typically have high frequencies. Perhaps this person is confronting old healing issues, and it has lowered his or her energetic state. When they have been resolved, his or her vibration will return to its normal, higher level.

Also, as you know, no human is perfect. In general, the companions who complement you will be trying their best to better themselves and also progressing, in their own speed, on the spiritual path.

In time, you will be able to sense who has a higher frequency. This will become second-nature for you. We are also more than willing to help you with this, and with everything.

Meeting New Friends

We encourage you to create a new "family" of loving, energetically light people who are also advancing on their spiritual journeys. It is your birthright to be around light, loving frequencies in all forms, including the other humans in your company. This is our preference for you, but, of course, it is always subject to your choice.

We suggest you make a list of activities you love and that make your heart sing. Of these activities, which involve others? Which are joyful? This is a wonderful way to meet new friends. You will meet them while you revel in your common love for an activity. Do you see how this differs from meeting to talk about the horrible state of the world or other heavy topics?

You could form a group based on a common interest in angels, Archangel Metatron or this series of books.

Selecting interests from your heart, then taking steps to pursue them makes it easier to attract wonderful companions. Please ask the angels to help you with finding your new friends and being open to the results.

If you insist on staying home alone, there is only so much we can do. Please consider getting involved in some activities you enjoy. You can join these virtually, although you may prefer to be physically present when possible. We will inspire you, if you so wish.

Common Questions
How can I help low-vibration and resistant friends and family?

You cannot. Everyone is on his or her own path. You can only continue fearlessly with your own growth and ascension journey. Your efforts on your own behalf may inspire this person, or they may not. In either case, it is best to detach from any outcome and focus on your own process.

What happens to my loved ones if they keep resisting?

Many people are indeed following the ascension path, but are moving so slowly that you might not perceive any movement at all. Everyone will reach the higher realms in his or her own timing. There is no need to fear.

Forces of light are working extensively with those who extremely oppose ascension. These individuals may choose to continue resisting, and we must respect their free will. We counsel you to do the same, even though this might be difficult for you.

What happens if I let my old friends go but haven't met any new friends yet?

This is a common problem, and one that many of our students experience. They say, "Archangel Metatron, we have let go of our low-vibration friends. And now we are all alone."

We are not asking you to let go of all your friends. That is up to you. In some cases, you may find this necessary, and we understand that. We are compassionate about your situation.

Being temporarily on your own is a symptom that you are still raising your frequency so you can accept new, lighter friends. We counsel you to take advantage of this time alone to do more self-healing and raise your vibration even further.

The fact that you are lonely is a sign that you are still transforming. Spend more time in nature, meditating and doing the things you love. When you focus on being happy and enjoying life, loving friends are effortlessly drawn to you.

We know it is difficult, in the interim, when you have not yet established your healthier, lighter patterns. We encourage you to stay persistent and not return to your old friends because you feel alone. However, this, as always, is up to you.

Please refer to the advice above for finding new, lighter friends.

What if I feel terrible about letting old friends go?

We are not asking you to remove anyone from your life. We simply suggest that you pay attention to how you feel in each person's company. If some people consistently reduce your vitality rather than add to it, we advise you to spend more time with those who boost you.

Loyalty to long-term friendships is understandable, but we urge you to consider the impact on you of being around those who consistently bring you down. We would say this loyalty is perhaps misplaced. Friendships are meant to be joyful and fun, not something to be endured.

If you believe your old friends "need" you, this is an illusion. Everyone is on his or her own path, and everything is aligned in its misalignment, or perfect in its imperfection. We recommend that you allow your friend to find his or her own way and release the desire to be needed.

As stated above, not everyone is embracing the ascension process, and it is difficult for you to be around anyone who is resistant. Whether you decide to spend time with them anyway is, as always, your choice.

We suggest you open to light, happy friendships and accept nothing less. This is our preference for you.

As for feeling terrible about making the best choices for you, we remind you to never judge yourself in any way or for anything. It is damaging and counterproductive to do so. We do not criticize you from where we are. Please try to forgive yourself for all you believe you have done "wrong" in your life and move on to a happier, more loving future. We are here to help you with this and with everything.

What if I am isolated because of the recent pandemic and related world events?

This book was written during the 2020-2021 pandemic, and we are well aware of the issues involved.

It is a challenging time for many of you. Please know that you are never alone, and we are always there for you.

We would encourage you to stay active as much as possible and try to create your own personal reality of safety, love and trust. When you are ready, please take steps to remove fear from your energy system. You would benefit from the *Meditation to Dissolve Fear* in Chapter 6 (Maintaining Your Energy Integrity).

Try to connect with caring friends and family when possible, even if this is done virtually for now. Remember, you are seen and loved. No one has forgotten about you.

The situation is temporary and will not last forever. See it as an opportunity to reconnect with yourself, heal, enjoy nature, and spend more time with us.

We will not discuss the pandemic in this book other than how it affects you, as this is not relevant to your personal growth and next steps.

Romantic Relationships

So many of you are completely distraught over your romantic relationships. They are a source of great struggle and hardship for you. Many of you have allowed them to become blocks to your ascension process (please refer to the explanation of energetic guns in Chapter 4, Energetic Guns).

We are asked all the time, "How can I make my romantic partner come along with me into ascension?" Our answer is that you cannot. It is the same with friends and family members, which we discussed previously. No one can be forced into ascension more quickly than they desire. Each person is always in control of the speed of his or her own process. This is a sacred choice made out of immutable free will.

If you are in a relationship, we invite you to follow the foregoing advice on family and friends.

If you are single, we encourage you to do inner healing work on yourself before looking for a partner. We know this may be unappealing to you. But when you have transitioned into the lighter frequencies, you can easily attract a new partner with beautiful qualities and a high vibration.

We will help you intuitively know when you are ready to receive a new romantic partner. In general, it is when you are feeling good and happy around 80% of the time. We would never ask you to not be human, for that is what you are. You are not required to be perfect. Yet, when you reach the point of being in energetic alignment 80% (most) of the time, you are usually ready to accept romantic love into your life.

What to Look for in a Romantic Partner

It is important to disregard your previously held criteria for selecting a romantic partner. Instead, focus on the light feelings described in Chapter 4 (Removing Outdated Frequencies & Programming).

You also can consider these questions:

- Do I feel good around this person?
- Does the whole interaction feel like wellbeing, happiness and wholeness?
- Am I calm or agitated when I am with him or her?
- Do I feel a strong positive pull to this person?
- Am I sexually attracted to him or her?
- Is he or she usually cheerful or in a low mood?
- Are my heart and body both aligned in attraction to him or her?
- Am I at ease around this person's energy?

- Does it feel like I energetically open up in his or her presence, or does part of me seem to shut down?
- Do I feel happy or unhappy after being with him or her?

A high-vibration romantic partnership will feel positive, upbeat and fulfilling. It may be calm and dynamic at the same time. It is balanced and aligned.

We are not saying you should be searching for a "perfect" person. Just as you are human, your romantic partner will be, too.

Above all, we advise you to welcome a romantic partnership that FEELS like wellbeing. If it does not, then perhaps this person is not compatible with you, or maybe you are not yet ready to attract a loving partner. It is best to avoid relationships that have dominant lower frequencies, such as addictions and abuse.

Becoming Ready for Love

There are several ways you can prepare yourself to welcome the energy of romantic love into your being and life.

We suggest the following:

- Ask the angelic forces to help prepare you

for romantic love and to bring your partner to you.

- Consciously open to the energy of LOVE in all forms.
- Try to embrace the energies of FLOW and EASE.
- Know that you are worthy and deserving of being truly loved.
- Work with Volume 1 to release any pain from past relationships (or consult a professional healer).

We know it may be difficult to believe in this moment, but when you are truly ready for your romantic partner, he or she will appear. We counsel you to focus on yourself and on your own journey until your love arrives. Then you can begin to walk together.

Keeping the Faith

You may be ready for love, but your partner has not yet materialized in your life. This can happen. It is important to not feel frustrated, for if you do, you will only slow down the process. There is often a physical delay between when you have prepared for something and when it shows up.

To make this period more comfortable for you, we invite you to "borrow" our unwavering faith that what you have asked for (your romantic partner in this case) is on his or her way to you. You can also visualize already being with this person. It is crucial to keep the faith at this stage so as not to postpone his or her arrival.

These inner challenges may hinder you from establishing a loving relationship:

- Low self-worth or value
- Frustration
- Fear
- Disbelief or doubt
- Lack of trust
- Collective consciousness beliefs, like you're too old or "too" anything

We recommend that you open to a new perspective on these beliefs. Most importantly, we advise you to deepen your connection with the angelic realm. You will receive our assistance with your love life and many other benefits, such as an improved mood and energetic state.

"Twin Flames"

There is much distress about "twin flames."

People ask questions like these:

- How do I find my twin flame?
- Do I have one?

- Did I miss him or her?
- Was I excluded from this?
- Have I done something wrong, and now I don't get one?
- Is this certain person my twin flame?
- How can I get him or her to come back to me?

Soul relationships exist among you, and some are closer in nature than others. This is a fact. However, the twin flame relationship is a mythology. We prefer for you to let go of this concept and focus on compatibility, as discussed above.

Remember, nothing that causes you anxiety, fear or worry can ever be beneficial for you.

HIGH-FREQUENCY SEXUALITY

Sexual energy has historically been rife with lower frequencies, but it is changing. Some of you have already sensed this.

It is a beautiful, extremely powerful, life-giving force and yet many do not regard it as such. Upgrading your sexual energy and your perception of it is part of the new consciousness rising up on the planet.

Connecting to High-Level Sexual Energy

First, it is advisable to allow us, the Lord Metatron, to upgrade your sexual system at the cellular level (see instructions below). This upgrade increases your awareness and allows you to connect with others in a lighter, more heart-centered way. It will improve all of your interactions, not just those with a sexual aspect.

Second, discontinue any involvement with the old sexual frequency. We recommend seeing sexuality and love as one. It is vital to infuse, at all times, sexual energy with the heart's love and wisdom. We suggest you engage in all sexual activity in a loving and respectful way. Additionally, we advise you to abstain from sex that is purely physical in nature, with no emotional attachment. You will find this to be increasingly less satisfactory anyway as time goes on.

Third, focus on your state of mind. Sex is not meant to be a dirty secret. It is essential to re-frame your perceptions of it in a healthy, guilt-free way. Sex is an important communion with the Divine. It is time for it to be seen as the sacred act that it is.

Meditation to Upgrade Your Sexual Energy

1. Please find a comfortable place to sit quietly, where you will not be disturbed.

2. Take some deep breaths as you start to relax.

3. Set the intention, in your mind, to connect with our energy. If you like, you can repeat our name as a mantra in your mind: "Metatron, Metatron, Metatron."

4. Feel our love and sparkling white light all around you.

5. Allow this energy to merge with you, knowing you are safe and loved.

6. Breathe slowly, focusing on these feelings.

7. Set the intention to allow us to upgrade your sexual energy system.

8. Take some deep breaths.

9. Now focus your attention on your pelvic area. See it immersed in white light.

10. Feel the loving energy in this part of your body.

11. Visualize any lower energies floating away from it.

12. Breathe and allow this transformation. You may have flashes of past experiences, memories or trauma come to mind during the process, or you may not. Either way is perfectly fine.

13. Bring your attention back to your connection with us. Repeat the mantra with our name, if you like, and focus on our loving presence.

14. Notice the feelings of safety and peace we are bringing to you now.

15. Once again, see your pelvic area immersed in loving white light.

16. Take some deep breaths as you relax more and more.

17. Sit quietly until you intuitively feel that the process is complete. Do not worry if you are not sure, because you can always repeat this meditation again another time.

18. Mentally thank your helpers and guides from your heart for their assistance today.

19. Now imagine that you have tree roots coming out of the bottoms of your feet and extending deep into the Earth.

20. Visualize that you are in a super strong bubble of bright white light. This is a magic bubble, and only love can enter it.

21. When you are ready, you can begin to move your physical body and come back into the room.

There is a guided meditation for this upgrade here
www.kristintaylorintuitive.com/ascensionbook2
(Meditation 7, password: loveandmagic)

You may wish to practice this meditation daily for seven days or as long as you feel guided.

If you feel that some old memories have been brought up by this meditation, it may help you to journal about them or talk to a trusted friend. You are always free to consult a professional, and we do recommend this if you do not begin to feel better on your own (with our help, of course).

Your sexuality is simply another aspect of you that would benefit from being energetically upgraded. However, we would never seek to control you in any way. You are always free to make your own choices.

The Nature of High-Level Sexual Energy

High-vibrational sexual energy is very healing for both partners (and for yourself, if you are on your own). It enhances and deepens your connection to the Divine. A magical expression of love, this type of sexual activity opens a portal to the higher realms. Both parties are elevated to higher frequencies, which is extremely beneficial for them.

To better access these energies, you can take certain steps before, during and after making love or engaging in self-pleasure:

1. **Set the intentions.** You can set intentions to experience high-frequency sex in your life generally and also right before making love. If

you are with a partner, it is best if both parties do this, but not entirely necessary.

Say these firmly and powerfully, from your heart, either out loud or in your mind. You could write them down as well, although it is not necessary.

As a general intention, you (and your partner if he or she is willing) could state something like:

"I intend to connect to the highest, beautiful, loving, and healing frequencies in the universe when I engage my sexual energy."

Stating it once is sufficient, unless you would like to repeat it.

Each time before making love, you (and your partner) could state an intention similar to this:

"I intend for this lovemaking session to be divinely aligned to the highest, loving, and healing frequencies in the universe and to be a beautiful expression of the love between my partner and I."

2. **Have the appropriate attitude.** It is important to adopt a mindset of respect and love for your partner, as well as towards yourself, that carries through the experience.

3. **Open your heart center.** Your heart center must be open before making love in order to experience the higher sexual frequencies.

Here is one of many ways to do this:

Exercise to Connect with Your Partner's Heart

1. Sit facing your partner. You may wish to sit on the bed or on the floor.
2. Place a hand on your partner's heart center while he or she does the same to you.
3. Close your eyes and intuitively sense your partner's heart energy.
4. Take a few deep breaths in this position.
5. Open your eyes and thank your partner.

You can tune into your own heart in the same manner, if you are on your own.

4. **Cleanse your energy afterwards.** After sexual activity, it is a good idea to disconnect from your partner's energy when you feel ready. You can follow the *Shower of Light Meditation*, which you will find in Chapter 6 (Maintaining Your Energy Integrity).

These are suggestions and not meant to be a formula. We encourage you to follow your intuition about what is right for you.

Signs You Have Energetically "Infected" Your Sexual System

The basic human attribute of sexuality has been compromised, and it is being utilized to infuse your energy fields with lower energies.

You may be wondering how to tell if you have introduced lower energies into your sexual system. Essentially, this happens if you open to sexual energy in a low-vibration way. This could be through sex that is purely a physical release. It could be via pornography, which at this point in time always has a low frequency. Or it could be caused by excessive sexual desire without any loving feelings or heart energy.

When you absorb dense sexual energies, your entire energy field is corrupted. You may feel the urge to engage in much more sexual activity than usual. Additional symptoms could be restless or disturbing dreams, and difficulty accessing your heart and emotions. You could become largely sexually focused and feel drained. This is how many people, often men, slip into addictions to pornography and sex.

Sexuality is one of the strongest ways humans have been enslaved. We are not judging this in any way, for everything is aligned even in its misalignment. We merely assert that the time has come for new sexual energy, higher-vibrational and purer in nature, to be enjoyed on your planet.

Your sexual system will remain spiritually infected until you clear it. We are happy to assist you with this, if you so wish. We recommend the sexual energy upgrade meditation above. Any other spiritual work with us or that originates from the highest light will benefit you.

Common Questions

I enjoy porn. Are you saying I shouldn't watch it anymore?

We always encourage you to make your own decisions about everything. Our advice for those reading this book is to avoid the pornography that exists on the planet at this time. We assert that the detrimental energetic effects from porn far exceed any enjoyment you may receive from it.

I don't have a partner for sacred sex. What can I do?

Similar to when waiting for your new, lighter-energy friends to appear, there can be a gap in time between when you have decided to attract a new, high-vibrational romantic (and sexual) partner and when that person actually arrives in your life. We ask you to be patient during this period.

Perhaps it is a time to reconnect with yourself with loving and nurturing self-care.

The same advice applies here as it did for meeting friends. Follow your heart and engage in some new interests. This can help you meet someone special.

We advise against having sex with someone just for the sake of it. This would be counterproductive and would energetically harm you.

When interacting sexually with yourself, be sure to do so with love and self-regard. You do not need to have a partner to engage in high-frequency sex. You can take this time on your own to upgrade your energy and improve your mindset.

What if my partner wants to make love in his or her own way?

It would be beautiful if you could explore spiritually aligned sex together. If this is not possible, we would advise you to take the preparation steps listed above, but in reference to yourself only. You are able to control your own experience and connection even when you are with a partner. If you do, sex will be more loving and fulfilling for you, regardless of your partner's intentions. Your lover may be influenced by you at some point in the future, even without his or her conscious awareness.

Is it energetically important to be monogamous?
What about other non-traditional sexual practices?

Discernment is one of the skills you incarnated on Earth to learn. You came to experience the oneness of the universe (after temporarily forgetting your light) and learn how to navigate this expanse. You are mastering how to choose what brings you joy and contributes to your energies without detracting from them.

We encourage you to practice this skill of discernment when it comes to sexuality. We are, of course, willing to inspire you with our guidance if you so choose.

We remind you that not all practices are of benefit to you, especially as a sensitive and spiritually awakened being.

Is marriage important?

Marriage is a beautiful celebration of love between two individuals. It is a wonderful union of two souls who feel a deep connection with each other.

The angels are supportive of your choice and of the love between you and your spouse.

You have a right to decide, according to your free will, whether marriage is beneficial for you.

There is nothing wrong with getting married, and there is nothing wrong with not getting married.

It is for you to decide.

What about divorce?

The worst thing about divorce is that so many of you blame yourselves for it. There are, without exception, many factors involved. Perhaps one partner has gone in a different direction. Maybe what once was a compatible relationship has become the complete opposite over time.

Accept the situation and forgive yourself. Nothing, and we repeat, nothing is worth blaming yourself for. As one of our students, we ask that you release your past and what is holding you back, whatever that is.

To clarify, we have no objection to divorce. It is most important to do what feels right for you and have compassion for yourself if a relationship doesn't work out. You are learning, and you are on Earth for this exact purpose.

We are always by your side.

CHAPTER 6
Energy Management

Maintaining Your Energy Integrity

MANY LIGHTWORKERS AND wayshowers struggle with constantly feeling energetically drained and out of alignment. What worked for them to clear their energy fields in the past seems to not help anymore.

We hear your concerns. We will address some ways to take your personal healing and energy management to the next level so that you can feel better.

Keeping Yourself Energetically Clear

You are learning to manage your energy field, and this is part of your lessons on Earth. We are here to help you, and we have given you many methods for this.

These techniques from Volume 1 may be helpful for you:

- Energy Alignment (page 44)
- Cleansing Your Energy (page 47)
- Energy Upgrade (page 33)

We also suggest the following:

1. Spend time with angelic energy. The more time you spend with our light (and in the presence of any divine frequency), the more harmonious your life will be. Therefore, we request that you sit with us for a short meditation daily. You can meditate on your own or listen to a guided meditation.

2. Take care of yourself. Wellbeing produces more wellbeing. If you want to feel good and be healthy, it makes sense to look after your physical body. Healthy food, adequate sleep and time spent in nature all help you to achieve and maintain a high vibrational state of being. After some practice, you will automatically be drawn to those environments, foods and situations that are the most beneficial for you. For recommendations on healthy eating, please see Chapter 7 (Supportive Dietary Choices).

3. Call on your team of the highest light. You may always call on your own personal team of the highest light, including us, the Lord Metatron, to assist you with whatever you need. In addition to helping you generally, we can clear and improve the quality of your energy field.

Meditation to Connect to Your Team of the Highest Light

1. Please find a comfortable place to sit quietly, where you will not be disturbed.
2. Take some deep breaths as you start to relax.
3. Set the intention, in your mind, to connect with our energy. If you like, you can repeat our name as a mantra in your mind: "Metatron, Metatron, Metatron."
4. Breathe slowly.
5. Now state this intention, out loud or in your mind:

   "I call on a team of helpers of the highest light to assist me now and always. I fully trust in your loving guidance and support."

6. Feel your connection to these beautiful beings as you breathe. Know that you are completely loved and supported by the universe. Your personal team is always there for you and you can call on them at any time.
7. Mentally thank your helpers and guides from your heart for their assistance today.
8. Now imagine that you have tree roots coming

out of the bottoms of your feet and extending deep into the Earth.

9. Visualize that you are in a super strong bubble of bright white light. This is a magic bubble, and only love can enter it.

10. When you are ready, you can begin to move your physical body and come back into the room.

There is a guided meditation for this process here www.kristintaylorintuitive.com/ascensionbook2 (Meditation 8, password: loveandmagic)

This meditation does not need to be repeated unless you wish to experience the loving guidance and support from your team in a deeper way.

4. Let go of fear. We recommend that you continue to release fear. It will make a huge difference in how you feel and also in the quality of your energy field. Sometimes it might be helpful to address any fears before attempting to remove an energetic gun, especially if it is one that is significant to you.

As a student of Metatron, we ask that you eradicate all fear, whether personal, ancestral or originating from mass consciousness, from your energy field. We prefer for you to continue working with us until this has been achieved. Of course, this is, as always, your choice.

Meditation to Dissolve Fear

1. Please find a comfortable place to sit quietly, where you will not be disturbed.
2. Take some deep breaths as you start to relax.
3. Set the intention, in your mind, to connect with our energy. If you like, you can repeat our name as a mantra in your mind: "Metatron, Metatron, Metatron."
4. Imagine that the most beautiful, sparkling white light is all around you and integrating with your physical body.
5. As we merge our energy with yours, you will start to feel a deep sense of safety and comfort.
6. Breathe slowly as you focus on these feelings.
7. Surrender to the healing power of this white light.
8. Let go of any thoughts in your mind and relax into this energy.
9. Take a few deep breaths as you continue to surrender to our energy working with you. If you are fearful, try to not focus on those feelings right now.
10. Allow us to bring into your energy field the

frequencies of safety, security, peace, comfort, and love. Just rest and allow this process.

11. Observe any fear you still have in your body melting away.

12. Feel the loving, positive energies taking up more and more space within you.

13. Imagine you are breathing in these positive, beautiful energies one at a time: safety, security, support, peace, comfort, and love.

14. Relax, let all of your thoughts go, and breathe deeply.

15. Feel the changes in your energy field.

16. Mentally thank your helpers and guides from your heart for their assistance today.

17. Now imagine that you have tree roots coming out of the bottoms of your feet and extending deep into the Earth.

18. Visualize that you are in a super strong bubble of bright white light. This is a magic bubble, and only love can enter it.

19. When you are ready, you can begin to move your physical body and come back into the room.

Please find a guided meditation for this here - www.kristintaylorintuitive.com/ascensionbook2 (Meditation 9, password: loveandmagic)

You may wish to practice this meditation daily for as long as you are still fearful. It can be repeated as many times as necessary.

Other Ways to Ensure the Integrity of Your Energy Field

Although we are always with you, sometimes creative visualization can allow you to feel our love and support in a more tangible way.

The more you practice maintaining the quality of your energy field, the easier it becomes. In time, you will not need to employ techniques such as these.

For now, the methods below may help you during challenging situations.

The White Light Bubble

Ask the angels to place you in a bubble of white light. Only love and the highest light can enter and leave this bubble. It is even more effective if you make sure you are grounded, imagining tree roots extending from the bottoms of your feet into the core of the Earth. Please refer to the *Bubble of White Light Meditation to Release Dense Energies* in Chapter 4 (Removing Outdated Frequencies & Programming).

The Triple Violet Flame - Archangel Shield

Imagine that you have a ring of archangels surrounding you on all sides.

Visualize a violet flame (a burning violet-colored spiritual fire) encircling the archangels.

Imagine there is a bubble of white light, the same type as above, enclosing the violet flame.

Archangel Buffer

If you are in a difficult conversation, imagine there are archangels between you and this person. Feel their strength and loving presence.

Cloaking

Sometimes those resisting ascension are hostile or aggressive to anyone who is actively raising his or her vibration. Without your conscious awareness, your light can cause some people to feel pressured or angry towards you. They may even target you with unkind behavior.

At your request, we will "cloak" you from these individuals and every being that is associated with them (meaning their helpers and guides). You may ask us in your mind, as often as you like or before you meet with these individuals. Depending on your vibrational level, you might find it beneficial to renew your cloak at least once a day.

This is a temporary measure because, once you transition into the higher frequencies, you will naturally be "cloaked" from all lower energies, without any effort on your part. Until then, this technique can support you while you continue with your ascension process.

Shower of Light

Another simple but effective way to cleanse your aura is to stand under the shower and imagine it is spraying beautiful, cleansing white light. You can do this while taking a real shower or imagine you are taking one, according to the instructions below.

Shower of Light Meditation

1. Please find a comfortable place to sit quietly, where you will not be disturbed.
2. Set the intention to connect to the Archangel Metatron and your team of the highest light.
3. Feel their loving presence all around you.
4. Imagine that there is a giant shower head above you and visualize white light pouring from it.
5. Allow the white light to rinse away anything that is not for your highest good and release it into the Earth.

6. Remain in the shower of light for as long as you like, allowing it to replenish and nourish you.

7. Mentally thank your helpers and guides from your heart for their assistance today.

8. Now imagine that you have tree roots coming out of the bottoms of your feet and extending deep into the Earth.

9. Visualize that you are in a super strong bubble of bright white light. This is a magic bubble, and only love can enter it.

10. When you are ready, you can begin to move your physical body and come back into the room.

You will find a guided meditation here -
www.kristintaylorintuitive.com/ascensionbook2
(Meditation 10, password: loveandmagic)

You can repeat this meditation whenever you like. It is a good practice to use on a daily basis, if you wish.

In time, your energy field will become stronger and you will not need to employ any energy-management methods. For now, take your time and refer to these techniques when necessary.

SELECTING A PROFESSIONAL HELPER

Everyone is on his or her own path out of the 3D and into higher vibrations. As you know, some are moving faster than others.

In current times, many advisors, healers and other helping professionals, some extremely well known, are unaware of their spiritual influences. They are accidentally engaging with "sticky" energies that seek to stop humans from reaching their true potential.

Some healers and spiritual mentors, despite intentionally calling on the highest light, end up drawing from "mixed" (high and low) energy sources for their work. This is beyond their awareness and due to their own unresolved healing issues.

Seeing such a practitioner can indeed affect your energy field.

We would never intend to incite fear over this or anything else. We bring it to your attention for purposes of your own empowerment. If you do find yourself feeling fearful, you could try the *Meditation to Dissolve Fear* in the previous section.

Tips for Choosing a Healer, Spiritual Mentor or Other Professional Helper

Ideally, we would ask that you only see those practitioners who have extensively confronted their own issues. Further, it is important that they know how to and do work with clear divine energy in their client sessions.

You can gauge whether this is the case by how you feel. Tune into your heart and your physical body in reference to seeing this professional. If it is beneficial for you and indeed a step forward on your path, then you will feel light and uplifted in your heart when thinking about it. The sensation will be similar to when you meditate with us: 100% positive, aligned and "right." It could help you to refer to the positive feelings listed in the section on choosing lighter energies in Chapter 4 (Removing Outdated Frequencies & Programming).

Here are some criteria for selecting a helping professional:

- Experience assisting others in a professional capacity
- Positive energy and attitude
- Warm, caring and loving
- Heart-centered, radiates love and is aligned in her or himself

- Authentic in demeanor and in communication
- On a spiritual path in his or her own right
- Respectful of your sovereignty and free will
- Not controlling or overpowering

The overall feeling of working with this person should be joyful and loving.

If a professional makes you feel stressed or anxious at any point, it would be a clear sign that seeing this person is not good for you. Another indicator would be if the helper seems to have fear-based or limiting beliefs. Sometimes healers have unresolved issues themselves that can get in the way of their client work.

You can always ask us for signs that seeing this practitioner is advantageous to you. You do not have to rush your decision. Take your time and feel your way through it.

Please note, however, that if you are scared of moving forward or getting help, you might have a sense of dread that could be confused for a negative feeling about a professional. In this case, it is useful to spend more time with us in meditation so that we can bring clarity, ease your fears and guide you.

Selecting a Practitioner Who Is Not Aligned With You

If you inadvertently choose a professional with imbalanced energies, it can still seem positive to see him or her, at least initially. You might even leave the session feeling good. Yet, this does not last. There is a type of "hangover" at some point afterwards, and you may not truly feel like yourself for a few days or longer. This is a sign that seeing the practitioner was not in alignment with your highest good.

Please take care to not confuse this situation with the possible aftereffects of healing. When you have had a healing session, you can sometimes feel a little low while you process the issues that have come up. This is perfectly normal.

If you see a practitioner who is not aligned with you and with the next steps in your life, do not worry. The situation is still "aligned in its misalignment." You will learn your lesson about discernment, and will probably choose differently next time. As always, forgive yourself for any "mistakes" you have made. You are progressing and developing your awareness.

If your energy field has been adversely affected, please call on us for assistance. You might benefit from listening to a guided meditation with us to restore your vibration.

CHAPTER 7
Food & Health

SUPPORTIVE DIETARY CHOICES

EVERYTHING YOU INGEST affects your level of vibration. It is a good idea to pay attention to what you eat and drink as much as you can, without stress or worry. Gentle changes can make a huge difference. As always, self-care and love are paramount.

If you wish to better access the higher realms, it makes sense to eat in a balanced way. Modern spiritual doctrine largely under-emphasizes the importance of your physical body, health and wellbeing. This is a misunderstanding. Your connection to the Divine is also found in your body, and even in its routine functions, which are sacred.

If you are following the ascension path, your body will eventually match your elevated vibration, but there are steps you can take to make the transition easier. We suggest paying adequate attention to the physical side of you.

Common Questions

Should I be a vegetarian to best enhance my spiritual growth?

The planet has long hosted a meat-producing and consuming society. We know this is a long-standing tradition for all of you. We are not asking you to abstain from meat. This is a decision you must make for yourself.

If you decide to refrain from eating meat, there will certainly be benefits to your health and vibration. This is what we would recommend for you. In time, none of your Earth citizens will consume it, and animals will be honored for their company and love.

We realize, however, that the Earth is still transitioning, and some of you may wish to continue consuming meat. This is your choice to make.

Which foods are best for me?

We advise you to follow a balanced diet with plenty of water, fruits and vegetables. Freshly prepared food is better than that which has been "processed," meaning it has been put together by someone else.

Remember to take into account the vibrational level of the person who has made your food. If you prepare it at home yourself or eat at a high-vibrational restaurant serving the equivalent of home-cooked food (yes, they do exist), then your food will benefit your body. "Fast food" and processed food does not add to your health and wellbeing.

Here are some factors to consider when selecting your food:

1. **Is this food fresh?** We mean as fresh as possible and not necessarily "organic" in each instance. In general, we prefer for you to eat freshly prepared, whole foods, instead of processed, as often as you can.

2. **Is it nourishing?** In other words, does it have nutritional value? Is it adding to your energy levels or detracting from them? This can be determined by known nutritional principles and your intuition. We can inspire you if you so wish.

3. **Is it prepared with care?** If you made it yourself, were you angry or upset when you prepared it, or content and peaceful? If you are eating at a restaurant, is the general feeling of the environment happy and loving, or harsh and fast? If you consider these questions, you

will be able to determine if your food was cooked with care and (ideally) with love.

We do not wish to cause any stress or inconvenience for you. It is necessary to consider what you are putting into your body, for it becomes a part of you. With everything you eat, it is worth considering that this will take place.

We encourage you to drink enough water as this is essential to continue raising your vibration and progressing with your spiritual development.

How do I best clean out my body and accept the higher frequencies?

If you are eating whole, nourishing foods as described above and drinking sufficient amounts of water, you are well on your way to preparing your body and energy field to receive the higher frequencies.

You may wish to consider limiting your consumption of meat and fish, but, as we stated above, this is your choice.

In some cases, "cleanses" or "detoxes" can be beneficial, depending on the program. In general, though, there is no need for them. Of course, if you feel drawn to such a regime, we invite you to trust your intuition.

Old pain and trauma can also hold unwanted

space in the physical body. We recommend taking steps to release it by following the procedures in Volume 1 or by seeing an appropriate professional.

What about food sensitivities and allergies?

Many of you ask us about your food intolerances, sensitivities and allergies.

We assert that these symptoms are never about the food itself. This may surprise some of you, but there is always a deeper issue causing the sensitivity or allergy.

We are happy to assist you with this. Also, it would benefit you to see a healer who can address this type of concern.

Of course, it is important to avoid ingesting anything that irritates your body in any way.

What about dairy and animal products other than meat?

Animal products, like those made from dairy, are not designed to be ingested by humans. Yet, they are not necessarily harmful for the human body in and of themselves, when consumed in moderation.

Many of you enjoy a variety of animal products. We do not discourage you from taking pleasure in them. We ask that you make your own decisions about what is best for you.

Is it better for me to eat vegan and not ingest animal products of any kind?

It depends on the person following this type of diet. Veganism has become so popular. But sometimes vegans, like many others, eat in a certain way to cover up healing issues they do not wish to address. We suggest that you look at all underlying energies influencing your behavior. As always, we are here to help you, with this and with everything.

Let's look at some examples of individuals and their diets:

1. **Person A** follows a strict vegan diet and also avoids many other types of foods. He feels a strong need to control his personal life, and his diet is an extension of this.

2. **Person B** eats a wide variety of foods, including meat, fish and dairy products. She is taking steps to release her painful past and working with us daily to move forward in the best possible way. Her diet isn't perfect, but she does what she can to eat home-cooked or carefully prepared foods that nourish her body.

3. **Person C** follows a vegetarian diet most of the

time, but also allows for her favorite non-vegetarian foods once in a while. She loves life, and it keeps getting better daily.

4. **Person D** is a vegan and extremely careful with what he eats. His health has improved, and his mood is high.

Which person's vibration is higher?

You might be surprised. We would say Person C, because she is eating a high-frequency diet that allows her flexibility to ingest what she prefers. She is not anxious or worried about what she eats, and she is making efforts to follow a healthy, balanced diet. She also has a positive attitude, which would increase her wellbeing.

A close second would be Person D and after that Person B, who is making great progress with improving her wellbeing. The concern with Person D is that he is following a rigid diet and not listening to his body. With Person B, she might be eating too many animal products, and this could adversely affect her body and vibration.

Out of these examples, Person A has the least healthy diet. His need to tightly control his food choices is a symptom of deeper emotional issues. Once they have been healed, he can move forward in a healthier and happier way.

Does it hurt me if I have caffeine?

Large amounts of caffeine interfere with your ability to receive the energies of calm and peace. It can also make it harder for you to connect with us and sense our guidance.

Even small amounts of caffeine could disrupt your body and energy field, if you are very sensitive. As you progress on your spiritual path, you may find you are less able to tolerate it, but this may not be the case.

It is our recommendation that you avoid ingesting a great deal of caffeine on a daily basis. As with everything, this is your choice.

Does drinking alcohol lower my vibration?

We never tell you what to do, but we have been asked a question. So we will answer it.

Binge drinking (having many alcoholic beverages in one sitting) is not good for you or your energy field. It is difficult for you to manage your energetic state after so many drinks.

We advise you to limit your intake to no more than three alcoholic beverages in one time period. You can ask for angelic help to maintain your energy integrity before you begin drinking. We also advise you to clear your energy afterwards, using some of the cleansing techniques in

Chapter 6 (Maintaining Your Energy Integrity). The *Shower of Light Meditation* would be beneficial for this purpose.

We know that daily energy management can seem like a chore, and yet it is so essential. First, and most importantly, it is vital because it is a critical skill you are here to learn. Second, it is important because of the "mixed" energetic environment you are exposed to daily while the planet lightens. Using these techniques will not always be necessary.

We recommend that you drink alcohol no more than perhaps two or three times a week. We wish for you to refrain from doing any energy work when you have been drinking. Please wait until you are in your natural state, without the influence of substances, before connecting with us. Know, however, that we never leave your side.

Our preference would be that you do not drink alcohol at all, but we know this is a great deal to ask of you in the current planetary environment.

Some of you believe that consuming red wine is healthy, and we understand this position. There are some scientifically proven benefits of drinking red wine. Yet, we assert that the advantages do not outweigh the disadvantages. If you enjoy it, by all means continue to do so, but we do not recommend ingesting it daily. Please refer to our recommendation above of having alcoholic beverages two to three times a week, at a maximum.

If you feel the need to drink alcohol more often than that, you are either experiencing healing issues or not connecting effectively to the higher realms. We can assist you with both of these. You may find the information in the section on drug use (below) helpful to consider in relation to drinking.

Does smoking harm my energy field?

It is a well-known fact that smoking tobacco is harmful to the human body. It makes sense that it also damages your energy field. Smoking does not add to your wellbeing or your ability to connect with us. It is best to stop smoking as soon as you can, and there are many tools to assist you with this. We are also here for you, as always.

What about recreational drug use?

Many of you have used drugs to escape your emotions and painful feelings. We understand why you would do so. However, we encourage you to see a professional who can help you confront the underlying reasons for this behavior. We are also more than willing to support you.

Some of you have used drugs to relieve stress and have fun. Perhaps your friends do it, and you feel the need to join in. You may not immediately see this, but it is also a way of covering up deeper pain.

Why do you have so much stress? Perhaps you hate your job. Maybe you are not managing your energy efficiently, and you are not balanced. You could have an unhappy relationship or family life. These are all factors to consider.

If you are using substances to have fun, what are the other ways you can enjoy yourself? We assert you are not truly connecting to the energy of fun if you are trying to access it through drug use. Let us help you to experience what fun really feels like.

It is common to take drugs because your friends do it. In this case, you might have a strong need to belong with others. This is another inner challenge to address.

If you no longer use drugs, but you have turned to them in the past, it is still worth assessing the foregoing paragraphs to see if any of the information relates to you.

Many people find that working with us feels so good that they no longer need to ingest any substances. This is our intention for you.

We are often asked about marijuana use. You are always free to make your own choices, and we would never criticize you for this. Yet, it must be said that any form of substance does alter your decision-making and level of clarity. It also impacts your receptivity to us. We prefer a pure connection with you.

As for spiritual drugs like ayahuasca, there is a time and a place for them to be of benefit to the user. For those following the Metatronic approach to ascension, we recommend that you do not take this type of drug. There is no need or purpose for you to do so.

Embracing Good Health

Many of you are concerned about your physical health, and this creates much fear, worry and stress for you. We completely understand and sympathize with this, as we do with all of your concerns.

We invite you to start seeing your health differently. Just as the universe is fluid and always changing, so is your health. Therefore, it is possible, and even likely, that you can begin to enjoy an increasingly better physical state.

As a result of your work with us to let go of the old and upgrade your energy system, you will begin to feel better. Many of your ailments may start to disappear, if you let them. It is always your sacred free will to continue to experience poor health. Yet, the "natural" state for a student of Metatron (which you are) is for your health to improve on a continual basis. We invite you to embrace wellness now.

You may have past trauma and emotional pain that are contributing to your health challenges. If so, we suggest that you let it go in the usual way, with the help of Volume 1. Of course, we are by your side every step of the way.

If you are sick and not getting any better, please accept our deepest compassion and love for your journey. But also know that life can be very different for you. You already know this on some level. Try to notice incremental improvements to your health and believe that they are really happening. You could also see if you resonate with any of the feelings associated with a "dark night of the soul," because this could be the case for you (see Chapter 3, Surrender).

You may not trust us when we say that everything is energy, and that it all, without exception, can be changed. You have had the experience of releasing your past when following along with Volume 1. You have thus felt how emotions can transition from unpleasant to neutral, or even to a positive state. The same kind of transformation can happen with your physical body, if you allow it.

The higher frequencies you are accessing through the process of ascension do not include that of illness and disease. We are in no way blaming you if you are sick in some way. We do suggest that you engage in further healing practices, either on your own (with our help) or with a professional.

The Importance of Physical Movement

Your human body is designed to move, yet plenty of humans disregard this fact. People often spend their days sitting at desks, without enough physical movement. Many are constantly in front of screens, eating unhealthy foods. If this is the case for you, then it is understandable if you do not feel your best.

We recommend that you make physical activity, in whatever form, a part of your daily life. This will help you to move energy and to stay in the flow of the universe. Nothing is meant to be stagnant, especially you.

You can choose whatever form of recreation you like, whether it be dancing, fitness classes, lifting weights, walking, or something else. It is important to choose something you enjoy. Perhaps you would prefer a variety of activities.

Common Questions

Some of my friends and family members are in poor health. What can be done for them?

We explained in Chapter 5 (Family & Friends) that your friends and loved ones are on their own paths. There is nothing you can do to assist them with having better health. When they are ready, they will accept the higher frequencies, in their own way and at their own pace, which may be considerably slower than your own. They will find the right helpers and receive the appropriate support, when the time is right. For now, it is important to observe, rather than worry about, their progress on their journeys. We understand this can be extremely difficult for you, and we are here to comfort you at all times.

I am overweight, and this never seems to change. What can I do?

This is indeed a common issue for many of you right now. Some of you have excess body weight despite your best efforts. We know this can be challenging, frustrating and upsetting for you.

In addition to eating healthy, wholesome foods and getting plenty of exercise, we recommend attuning to us in meditation, daily if possible. You likely have subconscious fear and a difficulty releasing that which does not serve your highest good.

When you feel ready, regularly practice letting go of anything that is no longer good for you or that you do not need. We recommend the *Meditation for Spiritual Surrender* in Chapter 3 (Surrender). We also suggest that you listen, as often as necessary, to the *Meditation to Dissolve Fear*, found in Chapter 6 (Maintaining Your Energy Integrity).

There can be other energetic reasons for excess weight, including the following:

- Not feeling safe in the universe
- Wanting to hide or be invisible
- Eating too many unsupportive foods for feelings of comfort and "love"
- Not feeling loved, seen or cherished
- Subconsciously choosing to adopt ancestral tendencies to be overweight

Connect with us often and receive the energies of safety, peace and security. You would also benefit from working further with us to release pain from your past. which can be done by following the procedures in Volume 1. If you have already done this, perhaps go through it again or enlist the support of a professional helper to assist you with any upsetting memories and trauma stored in your body.

I have recovered from a serious illness. I am very involved with organizations that help others who have it. Is this detrimental to my wellbeing?

When you have a particular illness or health condition, you are a vibrational match to that condition. Also, without your conscious awareness, your soul may be seeking to teach you certain lessons through the experience of being sick (see Chapter 2, Earth School). Or you could be experiencing a "dark night of the soul" (see Chapter 3, Surrender).

Whatever the reasons behind your health issue, when you have it, you are in line with its vibration. We could say that you are one with it, energetically speaking. When you receive treatment, and recover from the illness, you naturally distance yourself from it.

It is kind of like the break-up of a romantic relationship. At one time, you were very close. Then the relationship ends, and you begin to have more and more physical and emotional space. It is the same when you recover from being sick. This space is beneficial for you. It helps you get well and reclaim your good health.

So, when you are seeking to be truly healthy again, we recommend that you fill your mind and your days with exactly that: thoughts and experiences related to being well. Think of everything you do as either adding to you or taking away from you. Then consider, what is bringing you wellbeing today? What is the next step you can take in your life that will bring you closer to your goal of being healthy? Maybe it is a walk in the fresh air, or perhaps a guided meditation. Perhaps it is seeing a professional helper of some sort, starting a fitness routine, reducing your alcohol intake, or following a new eating plan. There are so many beautiful ways to enhance your wellbeing! We love all your efforts to be happy and healthy, and we completely support you in this. We are with you every step of the way, and we applaud every bit of progress you make, even if it is small in your eyes.

We do not recommend being involved with any groups or organizations that are related to the illness you experienced. Your participation would "rekindle," so to speak, the old energy of being sick. It would bring you back into alignment with having that particular malady, which we understand is what you do not want. So, we advise you against serving as a spokesperson, representative or another role for an organization focusing, in any way, on the illness you had.

Similarly, we do not advise you to coach or mentor others who are going through what you did. We know this may sound extreme, but it will be too difficult for you to resist entangling your energy once again with that of the sickness. It is very easy to identify with those who are having a similar experience to what you had and reignite all the same energy within you.

If this is not what you want to hear, we gently suggest that you have not yet released all the trauma and shock of being sick. You may even still be angry at the illness itself or offended by it. Perhaps your loved ones have died from the same condition, or it has affected many around you. This is a completely understandable reaction, yet be aware that all of these feelings tie you to that particular disorder.

When you have fully let go of the experience of being sick, you will not want anything to do with the illness or any of its related organizations. You will be much more interested in moving forward with your life in a beautiful way.

Allow us to help you reach this place. If you are having difficulties, as always, you can utilize the processes in Volume 1 or see a professional helper to work through your feelings and heal your painful experiences.

It could be an energetic gun if you need to be part of a certain organization or help others who have a particular illness. We can help you to remove these (see Chapter 4, Energetic Guns).

CHAPTER 8
Your Financial Life

MONEY

THE ENERGIES OF scarcity and lack are rampant on the Earth. They are so predominant in your culture that we understand why it can be difficult for you to believe in financial abundance. Yet, that's exactly what we will ask you to do from this point forward.

You see, your mindset exclusively determines how much money you have in your bank account. Your wealth is not decided by any outside factors, such as the financial markets, politics or pandemics. It is set by YOU and no one else!

This is what you might call a "double-edged sword," meaning that you now know for certain, to the extent you trust our words, that no external factor can ever influence your finances. You understand, if you believe us, that you have the ability to positively or negatively affect your wealth. You can choose to live in a mindset of poverty, fear, lack, and scarcity. Or one of abundance, love, and happiness. The decision is yours.

However, if you agree that the power is within you, then many of you will be afraid that you have somehow failed and you do not deserve financial abundance. If it is in your responsibility, then you may feel embarrassed that you did not do it better.

We assure you that these feelings, while completely normal and acceptable, are not necessary anymore. You have not failed yourself or anyone else. You have simply believed the mass consciousness, which promotes the myths of scarcity, disempowerment and lack.

Healing a Lack of Love

So, you are probably asking, how do you move forward in abundance? Well, you have taken an important first step by reading this book and allowing us, the Lord Metatron, to assist you on your journey, which we are delighted to do.

We ask you to consider whether you only feel a lack of money, or if you feel a deeper lack of LOVE. We suspect the latter to be the case. It is important to know and feel that you have always been deeply loved. This is true even if you had a difficult childhood. You can now allow the love of the Divine Mother and Divine Father to fill you to overflowing with all the love in the universe. You never have to be starved of love.

If your parents were perfect in the human sense, which none are, they still could not have fully met all your needs for love. It is not humanly possible, and this is perfectly normal. So, even if you had exceptional parents, it is nonetheless a good idea to allow the Divine Mother and Divine Father to love you even more profoundly than you could ever imagine.

If you still have distressing memories from your childhood, we suggest you revisit the procedures in Volume 1. As for the love from the Divine Mother and Father, we will be bringing this to you from this point forward, if you would like us to do so.

Moving Into the Flow of Financial Abundance

Adjusting your energy field so that you receive plenty of love is crucial, but it is just the beginning. Now we will move on to address more issues related to your financial abundance.

Scarcity has been one of your favorite ways of punishing yourselves for generations. Therefore, most of you have had traumatic experiences related to a lack of money. If you are still upset by these, which is completely understandable, we recommend revisiting the healing processes in Volume 1.

Remember that you are always, and without exception, worthy of all good, including plenty of money. You deserve to have all of your needs, including financial, met.

Consider the following questions:

1. **Do you believe there is enough money for everyone in the world?** Consider the natural world. Start to notice the abundance of leaves, trees, rivers, and blades of grass. There is no lack in nature. It is exactly the same in the human world. Scarcity is a myth.

2. **Do you believe you deserve plenty of money?** Many of you believe there is always someone else with a greater need than you. Or that something about you makes you unworthy of receiving large sums of money. Let us help you reconsider both of these perspectives. We assure you that no one is more deserving than you, of every wonderful thing in the universe.

3. **Are you scared of loss and of not having enough?** If you are hoarding your money or possessions, you are too afraid to let go and be in the flow of the universe. Money comes to those who relax into its vibration. Fear and worry repel it from you. One good way to begin letting go is to take steps to de-clutter

your home, removing old possessions and clothing which no longer serve you. We also recommend that you heal your anxieties about money, and we are happy to help you with this, if you so wish.

4. **Do you believe the world is doomed?** Especially with the pandemic happening at the time of writing this book, many of you believe that all good has been taken away from you. We know it is not enjoyable to be kept apart from your loved ones, have your leisure activities restricted, and be required to stay at home so much of the time. However, you are still safe, and you nonetheless live in an abundant universe. There is no real reason to believe otherwise. Please accept our help to shift your mindset.

Opening to a New Viewpoint on Money

We see all the problems humans have had with physical money and the perceived shortage of it. But you can change your perspective on financial abundance. We advise you to begin investigating all your beliefs and fears about money and finances. By looking within, you will find that your external reality changes more quickly than you might think.

Please be aware that scarcity mentality has been programmed into you so that you will stay in the 3D world. We are helping you to remove these energies from your consciousness (see Chapter 4, Removing Outdated Frequencies & Programming).

A poverty mindset also results from a lack of trust in the universe, and, often, from not feeling safe (see Chapter 3, Surrender). As you move into the ascension frequencies, you will also move into feelings of ABUNDANCE and PLENTY.

We are helping you to see the world through the lens of these energies, rather than lack and scarcity. This is a natural progression on the ascension path. We recommend you intentionally practice this mindset.

Feeling the Energy of Money

We invite you to receive the energy of money with open arms. Many of you believe that money is bad in some way. It is not. It is purely an organized form of energy exchange between humans, with no inherent "goodness" or "evil." It just IS.

With this in mind, we suggest you become curious about the frequency of money, as if you have never seen it. We also recommend that you connect with it regularly. The more you interact with money in any capacity, the more you will invite it into your life. Receiving financial abundance can be as easy as you allow it to be.

DIVINELY ALIGNED WORK

Just like everything else in your life, your commercial ventures must be aligned with the new ascension energies for them to be successful.

Working in a job you hate will soon be a thing of the past, and more fulfillment will be rampant on your planet. Businesses that operate in the old regime will no longer be viable going forward. We are telling you this so that you can be prepared and begin to move into these energies consciously. We are with you always, every step of the way.

How to Ensure Your Job is Divinely Aligned

Only employment that is divinely aligned with who you are will be able to continue into the future. We recommend that you assess your job accordingly to see if a change, at the appropriate time, is best for you.

We will now assist you with this evaluation.

First, ask yourself, are you truly happy doing this job?

- Does it make your heart sing?
- Are you happy and fulfilled by it, at least a majority of the time?

Certainly, it is normal for daily stresses to impact you. If, however, most of the time you do not enjoy your job, it is time to consider a new direction. We will assist you with finding one, should you so wish.

If you are mostly happy with your work, ask, is it aligned with the divine energies?

- Does your work help others in some way or make the planet a better place?
- Is it honest?
- Does it contribute to the lives of those who pay you?

Answering the above questions will help you to determine whether it would benefit you to find a different job or become self-employed.

Many more individuals are starting their own companies. In the near future, we will see, to an even larger extent, the rise of the entrepreneur, who will usually be community-focused and solutions-oriented.

Business Success Through Ascension

For a business to thrive through ascension, it is important to think of its impact as a footprint. What kind of footprint is your company making? Is it treading lightly, with loving steps, or is it stomping and destroying all that come into its path?

We are not asking for companies to sacrifice

profit or make decisions that help others while damaging the business. We are simply notifying all commercial entities, their owners and stakeholders, that "inconsiderate" businesses will not last through the ascension process. This is a fact, and we cannot alter it for some, even if you ask us to do so.

Below are some questions to consider when thinking about starting new commercial ventures or in reference to an ongoing business:

1. Am I unnecessarily or disproportionately harming anyone? If so, is there a better and kinder option I could take? We are not referring to ordinary competition between companies or normal business conventions. We are speaking of those practices which are unethical or cause damage to others.

2. Is my company taking all reasonable steps to protect the environment? This is the same question as the first, but in relation to the planet and the environment. Ask, are there other cost-effective ways to achieve the same commercial goal? We are not suggesting that businesses go beyond what is currently advisable or possible for them. We are recommending that environmental and ecological concerns be taken into account in all commercial decisions. This is the way of the future and will soon be unavoidable.

3. Is my business adding to the planet in some way (via human connection, better health, happiness, or some other benefit) or detracting from it? The organizations that will thrive as ascension continues are those that uplift others and the planet. The time for commercial enterprises that detract from the whole has ended. The businesses of the future are heart-centered and positively affect others' lives. That is where the financial abundance lies going forward.

Example 1 - A loving café

Imagine there is a café providing a valuable service: food and drink to those who wish to ingest it. The customers are happy because they are seeking nourishment. The merchant is happy because he or she is seeking to sell it. If the owner or the employees are lightworkers, then we all know that not just food and drinks are on the menu. Happiness, joy and fun are also served with every order. We would say that our little café is divinely aligned, with or without the beautiful energetic additions to the meals.

Example 2 - Clothing manufacturing

This company sells clothing to consumers. The factory producing the clothing has difficult working conditions, and the workers are poorly paid, even by local standards. It creates a lot of waste, which is dumped wherever possible, without regard to proper protocol or sustainability. This factory was chosen by the company because of its low rates.

There is nothing wrong with making money, and we encourage you to release all resistance to allowing yourself to have plenty of it. But perhaps you can see that this example is not about money. It is about respect and concern for fellow humans and the planet.

In this instance, it would be advisable for the clothing company to only work with factories that pay fair wages for their countries and have acceptable working conditions. The company would be setting a standard for humane treatment. Similarly, it could choose to work with a factory that appropriately disposes of waste, recycling where possible. It is important to handle waste in a non-damaging, commercially viable way.

We are not judging companies or factories such as these. This is simply a wake-up call that inconsiderate and uncaring commercial practices that do not support the whole will no longer be tolerated in the new economy.

To clarify, we are not against big businesses or industry. It is a fact that considering the human and environmental costs in your business operations and commercial transactions will be necessary in the very near future.

Common Questions

Fully recycled options are not currently available in my industry. What do I do?

As we said above, you can only do your best and that is more than enough. It is sufficient to take into account the considerations listed above and to try to implement them as much as you can. Most importantly, please try to not be worried or stressed about these matters. We are always helping you, with this and with everything, if you wish for us to do so.

I am doing my best, but constant economic shut-downs make it impossible to earn my livelihood. What do I do?

We acknowledge and have so much compassion for the challenging period ongoing at the time of writing this book. We encourage you to stay optimistic as much as you can.

Consider the following:

- Is it the right moment to re-invent your services or commercial offering?
- Can you take this time to engage in more self-care and healing?

Also keep in mind the suggestions given in Chapter 4 (Energetic Guns) for staying in a high vibration during a pandemic or world disaster. The same advice applies in reference to your work life.

Would you believe us if we told you that it is possible to both progress and thrive during a world disaster? Indeed, it is. Remember that you create your own reality.

In trying times, it is truly the best advice to rely on your spiritual team, making the connection between us stronger. Take it day by day and rely on us for our never-ending support and love. We see you and honor you for all that you are.

CHAPTER 9
Conclusion

ONGRATULATIONS ON TAKING your next steps into the higher energies of ascension. You can make no better investment than in yourself.

It is important to remember that you are on your own path, and you will go at your own pace. You may need to revisit parts of this book or of Volume 1. You might think that you have released all the pain from your past, but then something will come up in your life to show you otherwise. The journey is not linear, and this is perfectly normal. Remember to never pressure yourself to be in any place other than where you are right this moment.

Whether you can believe it or not, everything is in perfect divine timing. There is a flow and an order to all in the universe. We ask for your consistent and continued attention to our guidance, beyond the words of this book, and to your journey, but without worry, fear or overwhelm. If you ever feel this way, please ask us to assist you and take a few days off from any self-development or healing. Working with us is meant to be enjoyable and never a source of stress.

However, we do ask that you progress on your path, referring to our insights along the way. If you choose to do this, and it is always your choice, we would say that you are indeed an ascension helper, or wayshower. The terminology is of no importance. What does matter is that you have come to this planet for a specific reason, mainly to light the way for others. You are forging ahead, while others hesitate and hold back in fear. This is a transitional time, one in which humans are facing their darkest fears and most painful memories. Many will realize they are in dysfunctional environments and begin to make drastic changes.

We ask you to embrace your role and pay attention to our prompts, which will become more obvious as you increase your intuitive abilities and work with us longer. Others are guided and inspired by the steps you take, without you even realizing it. They know which way to go because of your example, without ever having met you or knowing who you are. You reach them with your energetic vibration, which is felt by all on the planet and out into the larger universe.

We encourage you to keep going. You have a vital part to play as the Earth gets lighter and those around you begin to follow your lead. It will be a joyous sight to behold.

As always, we are grateful for all that you are and all that you do. You are seen, acknowledged and deeply loved. This is just one of the ways in which we communicate with you. We are always in your presence, and you are never alone.

With all of our love and deepest gratitude,

ARCHANGEL METATRON

Glossary of Terms

3D/Third-Dimensional/Lower/Old Planetary Energies: Frequencies that are remnants of how things used to be. They do not allow for all the possibilities that are available for humans at present.

3D Programming: All humans have been programmed to resist ascension and remain part of the old planetary energies. It is in what you call mass consciousness or cultural conditioning. Perceived as the unspoken "truth," it is quietly woven into the fabric of many of your television shows, films, news programs, books, and collectively held opinions.

Aligned in its Misalignment, Perfect in its Imperfection: This means seeing all the difficulties you have experienced as being perfect in their own way, because they have brought you to the place you are today. This concept can also be applied when observing others living out of alignment with the Divine and their Highest Good. It can help you to stay detached, allowing them to be on their own paths.

Dark Night of the Soul: A period of many things going wrong for you all at once. This often happens right before you surrender to the Divine and have a momentous breakthrough. What happens to you during this crisis is usually whatever it takes to encourage you to surrender completely.

Discernment: The ability to make choices that are in agreement with yourself (including your Higher Self) and with the Divine or the spiritual realms. It is an indispensable component of divine alignment. Without it, you cannot become or stay aligned.

Divine Mother: The energy or archetype of the most loving mother ever, who can love beyond human capacity, thereby easing old, painful memories and unhealed issues related to the biological mother.

Divine Father: The energy or archetype of the most loving father ever, who is protective, supportive and trustworthy. His love exceeds all human capabilities and can help to heal painful experiences relating to the biological father.

Divine Grace: A beautiful energy that can be received once a person has fully embodied the states of humility, surrender, sincerity, and respect for the Divine. It is a gift and not an entitlement. The power of grace permits you to access the higher energies of love, joy, happiness, and peace. It also allows for miraculous results that could not otherwise be achieved.

Free Will: The sacred, immutable right to make your own decisions for your own life.

Higher Self: The spiritual part of you that is in the higher realms and functions as a source of guidance for you.

Life Expression Energies: Energies you came here to express. These energies radiate out of you and positively affect all those in your path, helping them with what they lack in their own energy fields. This is a healing function that occurs even without your conscious awareness. When you work with angels and the higher realms, the effect is intensified.

Money: An organized form of energy exchange between humans.

Soul Interests: Interests your soul has chosen for a particular reason, whether to learn, expand or contribute. These are themes and types of activities you love and feel passionate about. They are always positive in nature and make you feel happy, content, fulfilled, and satisfied when you take part in them. They continually captivate your attention, often from a young age. Each person has up to three soul interests in a lifetime.

Team of the Highest Light: Your own personal team of Divine helpers that can be assembled at your command. We, the Archangel Metatron, are included in this team.

About Kristin Taylor

KRISTIN TAYLOR IS a channel, intuitive healer, author, spiritual mentor, and artist dedicated to helping others reach their highest potential, deepen their spiritual connections and live high-vibration lives.

A natural intuitive, Kristin was aware of her gifts from a young age. She began exploring energy work over seventeen years ago when she discovered Reiki healing. Her experience with Reiki (to the Master-Teacher level) inspired her to pursue further spiritual training, including other healing modalities, medical intuition, channeling, mediumship, and psychic development.

Kristin has personally experienced the impact that healing and spiritual work can bring to a person's life. She has had several chronic health conditions healed, life situations dramatically improved and emotional issues resolved.

She is an expert at channeling. Kristin has been working with her main guide, Archangel Metatron, since receiving a visitation from him in 2006. She loves inspiring others with angelic messages of hope, love and peace.

Kristin seeks to empower lightworkers. She is the founder of the Lightworkers Training Academy, an online school providing spiritual development and healing courses.

She is the author of the popular 2019 book, *A Practical Guide to Ascension with Archangel Metatron*. This is her second book.

Her work has been the subject of significant media attention and has been featured in the Gazette Telegraph, Evening Standard, Psychologies, Spirit & Destiny, Chat-It's Fate, and Eastern Eye.

Kristin is a qualified lawyer and worked for several years in corporate law in the City of London. She holds BA (in Studio Art), JD and LLM degrees. She speaks fluent French.

She is also a spiritual artist. Her paintings fulfill different energetic purposes, transforming and uplifting the energy around them. Kristin has extensively exhibited her artwork, which is held in private collections worldwide.

When she is not working, Kristin loves to be in

the forest or at the beach. She enjoys salsa dancing, fitness, traveling, knitting, and cooking.

Kristin is based in London, UK and works internationally. An American-British citizen, she is originally from Colorado Springs, Colorado. She has also lived in New Orleans, Perpignan and Paris.

To receive weekly updates and special channeled messages from Kristin, subscribe on her website:

🌐 **Website:**
https://www.kristintaylorintuitive.com

f **Facebook: Kristin Taylor Intuitive**
https://www.facebook.com/kristintaylorintuitive/

📷 **Instagram: Kristin Taylor Intuitive**
https://www.instagram.com/kristintaylorintuitive/

▶ YouTube **YouTube: Kristin Taylor Intuitive**
https://www.youtube.com/kristintaylorintuitive